MENDED IN A
BROKEN WORLD

Living with Peace and Contentment

Brad Bartlett

Address all personal correspondence to:
Brad Bartlett
411 Blowing Rock Blvd, Suite 158
Lenoir, NC 28645-4407
MendedByFaith2022@gmail.com

Individuals and church groups may order books from Brad Bartlett directly, or from the publisher. Retailers and wholesalers should order from our distributors. Refer to the Deeper Revelation Books website for distribution information, as well as an online catalog of all our books.

Published by:
Deeper Revelation Books
Revealing "the deep things of God" (1 Cor. 2:10)
P.O. Box 4260
Cleveland, TN 37320 423-478-2843
Website: www.deeperrevelationbooks.org
Email: info@deeperrevelationbooks.org

Deeper Revelation Books assists Christian authors in publishing and distributing their books. Final responsibility for design, content, permissions, editorial accuracy, and doctrinal views, either expressed or implied, belongs to the author. We consider it a great honor and blessing to collaborate in projects intended to advance the kingdom of God.

Table of Contents

Acknowledgements

First and foremost, I want to thank God for His invitation to salvation. Thanks also goes to my wife, April, who has been with me on this life journey for so many years and has inspired me with ideas and editing. A great debt of gratitude goes to my editor, Ben Godwin, and the staff at Deeper Revelation Books. They have been a remarkable blessing. Also, I have a great love and gratitude to John Kwaku Appiah who has been my father in the faith for such a long time. Without the wisdom, prayers and love from his family to mine, none of this would have been possible. Thanks to Dr. Fred Stapleton who saw me as somebody when I felt like a nobody. My gratitude also goes out to my fellow school teacher, Julie Curry, who kept telling me I should write. Appreciation goes out to Allen and Shirley Shifflet, Daryl McCuiston and Richard Harwood for their faith, encouragement and friendship. Additional special thanks go to my dear friends, Bobby and Lora Triplett, who have built me up with encouragement and love.

Endorsement

I deem it a great privilege to write a comment on this book *"Mended in a Broken World."* The title is apt and very simple. It explains how to have peace and contentment in this broken world we live in today. I have known the author, Brad Bartlett, for close to three decades and know his sincerity in serving the Lord. I believe this book has opened another door for Christians to see beyond the environment within which the Lord has saved and placed them—how to behave when we face challenges which seem too huge to get over.

I thank God for making it possible for the book to come out at last. It is very simple, practical to understand and practice. Brad does not discriminate, and he is a down-to-earth person. I hereby recommend every child of God grab a copy of this book.

Apostle John Kweku Appiah.
Faith Outreach Ministries
Ghana West Africa.

Introduction

If we will really admit it, we need help to manage and cope with our lives. Generally, help from friends, counselors, seminars, a fairly recent outpouring of self-help books, as well as web sites are available. Though most of us hope our lives and the world are getting better, the world doesn't seem to be doing too well. There are wars, famines, earthquakes, plagues and tsunamis, not to mention pollution, overpopulation, diseases and changing weather patterns. This description of the world has many parallel analogies to our own lives, if we will admit it.

I am not foolish enough to pretend this book has all the answers we need; however, I believe you will find some important questions which deserve *your own* personal answers. If you are willing to read further, please listen with *your own ears* and independently think through the concepts and principles portrayed within. If at all possible, please do not use the well-worn, often minimally substantiated pathways and patterns of thinking which this world and the media have forced upon us all. Actually, we are never really fully satisfied with other people's answers.

The modern media portrays Christianity as a hate group. This is often because those who call themselves Christians poorly represent Christ and the core tenants of Christianity. This is a sad truth. Don't put this book down because of your opinion of Christianity. After trying all the world has to offer, I have found some truth worth sharing. In the beginning, I was very uneasy at where it was found. Honestly, if you found the answers which genuinely satisfied your true, deep, inner longings, should it matter if they come from the Bible?

This book is written to be a series of discoveries which will encourage us to grow in the life-transforming and freeing concepts for the God of the universe's intended plan for life. The work of transforming our souls provides true peace, solid rock security and a way forward. This design offers us life and "life more abundantly," instead of a life riddled with the wounds inflicted by the world's ability to injure our souls and block our goals. When lived out, this life plan is able to carry us confidently through the storms and trials of life with our peace and security intact. Done well, it also creates in us the *joy of loving people*.

The goal of this book is to have you consider the pros and cons of cultivating a healthy, well-functioning *relationship* with God. This God-given design for life opens up endless possibilities for living a life greater than ourselves. The life offered by this plan is so much greater than a life where we are *in the center*. The self-centered life is surrounded by all the possessions and activities of this world which we suppose, if it is done "right," will give us the much sought after true inner peace and contentment. Yet honestly, in the quiet moments of our lives (which are so decorated and surrounded by all the best we can do in our own strength and striving) we still have this gnawing feeling that there is something missing. There is something more we want and need.

Additionally, let's face it, does it truly make logical sense to believe this entire world and the life we live is a product of chance? We know that everything around us eventually decays. So how could this world have fallen together to form something as precise and intricate as an eyeball or a brain? There is a place formed deep inside of us which longs to be filled. It is a God-shaped place (a hole in our soul) which is comparable to an exact puzzle piece which fits perfectly. It is a place which is custom-made for the living, life-giving God of everything. This place, when filled with the Creator and sustainer of the universe, illuminates our life like electricity through a light bulb. Without electricity, the light bulb cannot be truly "alive" or fulfill its purpose.

So, how do we move from our life, to the idyllic life previously described? It happens through inward change. Not a single one of the issues which trouble us deeply will change unless we first deeply change. Change and life go hand in hand. If you are alive, you change, either for better or for worse. Things that are dead do not change, unless life is added to them. For example, taking a blank, "dead" canvas and creating a painting brings the canvas to life and moves those who view it. Whatever does not have life just decays. When invited, God comes to us and offers the blueprints, tools, training and support needed to build something more magnificent and rewarding out of our lives than anything we could ever build on our own.

God, the Author of Life, offers true life, not just an existence. This sounds too wonderful to be true. And quite honestly many "Christians" struggle in their hearts to believe it *is actually true!* The transforming renovation we speak of has too often been made an intellectual exercise with rules, formulas and required behavior. It is often misrepresented by performance-based living and thinking. Thinking which goes like this: if the life-giving concepts of God's plan make *reasonable* sense, then they are *automatically* represented and practiced in my life. This attitude does not require inward change and thus creates a shallow plastic faith-life. The wonderfully designed plan functions well by submitting our life, our will and our choices to the life-giving principles and gentle guidelines of the *Spirit of the living God*. Amazing changes for the better will happen. The *caterpillar* will become a *butterfly* through this transforming metamorphosis.

All cultures and religions attempt to describe and define the creation of the earth and the supernatural. Even modern-day science attempts to describe these. So, my question is how do we move from our current understanding of life to the life God has for us? I sincerely began asking myself this same question several years ago.

After considering history and major literature of the world, I wanted to discover what early followers of Christ had which so upset one of the largest empires in the history of the world—the Roman Empire. Please consider this: The Bible is the most broadly published and widely read book in the entire history of literature. There is something inside this supernatural Book which has caused the mystery and controversy surrounding it. Whatever the mystery is, it is missing in many modern-day "Christian" churches. This became my daily prayer: "How do I become more like the early, New Testament believers?" So, with a healthy diet of sincere prayer and Bible reading, I journaled each step, each inward change, each lesson of circumstance and each revealed "eye opener." My journey is in no way a journey completed, but a living quest continued. Come whether you are a believer or an unbeliever; let's journey together as we electrify our lives and become "the light of the world" needed to illuminate an ever-darkening world. Let us attempt to discover truth, hope and contentment which we all need in greater measure as we become mended in this broken world.

CHAPTER 1

GOD DOES NOT PLAY FAVORITES

"For there is no partiality with God."
(Romans 2:11)

God loves everyone unconditionally. Love is the foundation of His creation. But here is the rub: God loves all His creation, which includes you and me, but He does not love sin (the behaviors that keep us apart from Him). He hates it because it cripples His plan to bless us and give us abundant life.

> *"I call heaven and earth to witness against you today, that I have set before you life and death, the blessing and the curse. So choose life in order that you may live, you and your descendants, by loving the Lord your God, by obeying His voice, and by holding fast to Him; for this is your life and the length of your days, so that you may live in the land which the Lord swore to your fathers, to Abraham, Isaac, and Jacob, to give them"* (Deuteronomy 30:19-20).

We love the Lord by obeying His Voice. We learn the language of His voice by studying His recorded Word. We "hear" Him by quieting ourselves in prayer and listening for His quiet, still, small voice. The world is loud and pushy. God is inviting and quiet. The land he swore to give in the above verse is a land of peace and plenty found by us as we live according to His ways. We cannot find the promised way by living according to our understanding of the world and our selfish nature.

> *The world is loud and pushy. God is inviting and quiet.*

Today we can live by His "voice" and enjoy the peace and plenty of a life lived according to His ways. On top of that, He will involve us in some incredible activities He is doing around us! We will not find this in what the world has to offer.

The working out of His plan invites us to life, an abundant and full life. Christ did not die for us to fall short, live in fear, hide from Him or deny Him. We also are not better off using whatever means the world has to offer to deal with the pain of life's trials and struggles. We are not to look for relief, but rather deliverance! His Spirit comes alongside and leads us to victory by reminding us who we are and whose we are.

> *"He who did not spare his own Son, but gave him up for us all—how will he not also, along with him, graciously give us all things? Who will bring any charge against those whom God has chosen? It is God who justifies. Who then is the one who condemns? No one. Christ Jesus who died—more than that, who was raised to life—is at the right hand of God*

and is also interceding for us"
(Romans 8:32-34, NIV).

So, are we going to follow the way God offers or are we content with our own unsettled ways? One thing is sure, a life tangled in our doing whatever we feel like is a sure recipe for the mess we can get in with what the world has to offer. God offers hope through a Spirit-led life. The world and its circumstances, surroundings and choices often drive us to battles with discontentment and even despair.

Reflections

1. Examine and explain how you feel about the concept of obedience to authority in your mind and heart.

_____

_____

_____

2. Recall occasions where you have been involved in something greater than yourself.

_____

_____

_____

3. Make a comparison of what you believe the world offers and what you think God offers.

_____

_____

_____

CHAPTER 2

MY WAY OR YAHWEH?

"For I am the Lord your God,
The Holy One of Israel, your Savior."
(Isaiah 43:3a)

Oh, how we need help! Before salvation when my self-driven ways and my own selfish desires, were the only option, life was weary from striving to attain what seemed to be a series of distant and confusing goals. God's ways were foreign to me, but by grace, He became my Lord and King. A wonder-filled life began. Also, the battle began ... the battle between the self-centered, earthly nature and the spirit man. Empowered by God and freshly rescued, we combine our efforts with God's power and truth and the much-needed renovation process begins.

After some time, we realize the benefits and blessings of growing closer to God and hopefully begin to hunger and thirst for His Righteousness. However, there remain thoughts, attitudes and actions we cannot seem to overcome even though we know they are displeasing to God. This is an important crossroad in our faith

After some time, we realize the benefits and blessings of growing closer to God.

journey. One way leads to holiness and the other way leaves us wandering around in the wilderness of worldliness.

Here is God's desire:

"So that He may establish your hearts without blame in holiness before our God and Father at the coming of our Lord Jesus with all His saints" (1 Thessalonians 3:13).

This important goal cannot be reached in our own strength. It requires the process of faith and action empowered by God. God specializes in doing what our natural man considers too difficult or even impossible. On the other hand, we may stay in our worldly ways and say something like "God understands, He knows I'm just that way." And thus begins Christianity with a limp, or even a crippled Christianity.

"And without faith it is impossible to please God, because anyone who comes to him must believe that he exists and that he rewards those who earnestly seek him" (Hebrews 11:6, NIV).

Do not be discouraged because Christianity is a growth process that requires faith. The salvation of true Christianity is not an event, it is a *process*. God will always enable you to take the next step He desires for you, but He may not enable you to take the next step you want to see happen. God is willing to take us as far as we are willing to go toward life and life more abundantly. It requires

His leadership, His Lordship, His timing and His training.

So where are you in this process? Have you even begun the process? If you have not begun, read on and give it some consideration. Considering the condition of our lives, it is worth investigating. Are you letting the Lord be the Captain of the ship of your life? The hope of heaven and assurance of getting there is strengthened by increased cooperation with God in reforming us to be more like Christ.

"And put on the new self, which in the likeness of God, has been created in righteousness and holiness of the truth" (Ephesians 4:24).

Reflections

1. Are there qualities in your character or habits you desire to see changed? List a few changes which you have not yet seen accomplished.

   _____

   _____

   _____

2. What do you feel or think would be a loving God's desire for your next step in the development of your life?

   _____

   _____

   _____

3. If you imagine your life being totally led by God, explain how it would be better or worse than your life today.

   _____

   _____

   _____

CHAPTER 3

COMPASSION IS COSTLY

*"For this reason it says,
'Awake, sleeper, and arise from the dead,
and Christ will shine on you.'"*
(Ephesians 5:14)

Lord, please deliver me from a cold, carnal, calculating heart which is focused on my comfort and not on the Comforter. So often we look at the circumstances of our life and start by applying the standards, observations and reasoning of this world to guide daily decisions. We must be relentlessly honest with ourselves to realize that often this dying world's standards guide us more than God's life-giving standards in our daily decisions. The carnal nature pushes us to achieve but God invites us to believe ... believe with our actions: His ways are best. The Word of God and God's Spirit instruct us in His ways as we read, pray and listen. Read the Bible regularly, pray regularly, and listen to reliable teaching regularly. Otherwise, this world will drown out the counsel of God in our decision making.

> *We must be relentlessly honest with ourselves.*

"And do not be conformed to this world, but be transformed by the renewing of your

mind, so that you may prove what the will of God is, that which is good and acceptable and perfect" (Romans 12:2).

Being compassionate is a pillar in the temple of God's will for us. Compassion is costly. Compassion costs us our time and our resources. Compassion cost Jesus His life, even though He went about doing good and restoring people who were oppressed by the devil. We are instructed to have compassion ... to "go and do likewise."

"'Which of these three do you think was a neighbor to the man who fell into the hands of robbers?' The expert in the law replied, 'The one who had mercy on him.' Jesus told him, "Go and do likewise"'
(Luke 10:36-37, NIV).

Jesus asked this question after He shared the Parable of the Good Samaritan. Compassion is costly. The world repaid Christ with crucifixion for doing God's will. In our efforts to allow Christ to shine through us and bring life to others, we will surely encounter struggles. This resistance, from the enemy of our soul, is manifested in many ways and is skillfully aimed at our weak points. But the joy of the Lord experienced while living God's Word and following His Spirit far outweigh the enemy's worldly attempts to discourage us.

"These things I have spoken unto you, that in Me ye might have peace. In the world ye shall have tribulation: but be of good cheer; I have overcome the world" (John 16:33, KJV).

We are to "rise and shine" for Christ. We are to turn away from the world's death-producing way of living which often leads to the death of our true hopes and dreams. There are overall callings from Christ, for example: love and compassion. When these are practiced, God will then guide you to a more specific calling. We will truly prosper greatly when we operate with obedience to the Lord in the areas of His general calling and allow our specific giftedness and calling to develop.

"This is a trustworthy statement; and concerning these things I want you to speak confidently, so that those who have believed God will be careful to engage in good deeds. These things are good and profitable for men" (Titus 3:8).

Reflections

1. List examples in your life where the world is drowning out the desires of God for your life.

    _____

    _____

    _____

2. If you had more compassion and love for people, how would that influence your attitude and wellbeing?

    _____

    _____

    _____

3. What do you feel in your heart is a specific calling or destiny for your life? This may be what you want to become on the inside or what you desire to do on the outside.

    _____

    _____

    _____

CHAPTER 4

A MATTER OF
LIFE AND DEATH

"For the mind set on the flesh is death,
but the mind set on the Spirit is life and
peace, because the mind set on the flesh
is hostile toward God; for it does not
subject itself to the law of God,
for it is not even able to do so."
(Romans 8:6-7)

Life and peace ... the abundant life ... are you feeling it? Are you experiencing it? Is it a reality for you? Let the old self-nature lead and it will lead to death. Let the new Spirit nature lead. This leads to life and peace. It sounds pretty simple. It is simple. However, it is not easy. In fact, it is impossible without the Spirit of God guiding you from within.

> *"So then, brethren, we are under obligation, not to the flesh, to live according to the flesh—for if you are living according to the flesh, you must die; but if by the Spirit you are putting to death the deeds of the body, you will live"* (Romans 8:12-13).

It gets complicated when we are not honest with ourselves about where we are in this thing called Christianity (being Christ-like).

This is eternally significant: Do you want to die in your flesh-led sin nature? Or, do you want to live by the empowerment of the Spirit of God? Life or death and good versus evil are the foundations for every book, every movie and every story ever told.

Historically, every culture has interpretations or belief systems that address the spiritual side of life and behavioral norms. Additionally, the world is full of opposites: up/down, left/right, cold/hot, light/dark ... the list goes on.

When it comes to light, there is an interesting aspect. You can add light to a dark room and it becomes light, but you cannot add darkness to a room which is lit and make the room dark. Light is superior to darkness.

"Then Jesus again spoke to them, saying, 'I am the Light of the world; he who follows Me will not walk in the darkness, but will have the Light of life'" (John 8:12).

Let this verse penetrate your soul. Do you have the Light of life guiding you? Or are you living a darkened life of stress, struggles and strife while worrying in your weariness?

Do you have the Light of life guiding you?

This battle between flesh and Spirit is most often lost by a failure to honestly admit where we are in this struggle. An intellectual agreement with Christianity and its principles does not transform your life or move you from death to life.

Measure yourself.

> "Now the deeds of the flesh are evident, which are: immorality, impurity, sensuality, idolatry, sorcery, enmities, strife, jealousy, outbursts of anger, disputes, dissensions, factions, envying, drunkenness, carousing, and things like these, of which I forewarn you, just as I have forewarned you, that those who practice such things will not inherit the kingdom of God. But the fruit of the Spirit is love, joy, peace, patience, kindness, goodness, faithfulness, gentleness, self-control; against such things there is no law" (Galatians 5:19-23).

Are you practicing what the world has trained you to do? Or, have you traded that in for what only the Spirit of God can guide you to become?

Reflections

1. What are your thoughts or hesitations about embracing the spiritual side to life?

    _____

    _____

    _____

2. Make an honest and personal list of your be-haviors or thinking patterns which "lead to death" in the context of the Bible verses above.

    _____

    _____

    _____

3. Explain why you do or don't believe that there is a God of the universe who wants to give you a better life?

    _____

    _____

    _____

CHAPTER 5

RESTORATION OR DEMOLITION?

"For He rescued us from the domain of darkness, and transferred us to the kingdom of His beloved Son, in whom we have redemption, the forgiveness of sins."
(Colossians 1:13-14)

Which of my sins are not under His blood sacrifice on the cross? Are there some He still holds against me and others He has forgiven? How silly that is! We are the ones who seem to select which of our sins, both past and present, are beyond His grace, mercy and forgiveness.

By this decision, we give the enemy ammunition to fire at us with his favored weapons of guilt, shame and condemnation, which makes us want to hide from God. We ought to run to a loving, healing, wonderful God. By His power and by our having a heart for Him, we will turn away from what is displeasing to Him. We tend to think in our perfectionist mindset, if we give more effort to doing better, then we will get beyond the fear of punishment. We must believe this truth concerning God's love for us:

"There is no fear in love; but perfect love

casts out fear, because fear involves punishment, and the one who fears is not perfected in love" (1 John 4:18).

Receive the perfect love demonstrated toward you by Jesus. Receive it and show it to others. Do we act like His sacrifice is only good enough or His blood is only powerful enough for some of our offensiveness toward Him? If so, we will cower in fear. He knows what we are made of, but He also knows what He can empower us to become.

If we begin to truly believe all our sins past, present and future are forgiven, then won't sin run out of control in our lives? Quite the opposite is true. This totally lifted sin burden births in us the desire to turn around, run from it and run toward God. We will not continue in it, dwell in it or call transgressions anything other than forgiven. The resulting reward of deliverance along with a more abundant life, which is provided by God and with our cooperation, creates a transforming courage to move away from our "stinkin' thinkin'" and behaviors which are disrespectful towards God.

With practice we give up on following the desires of our selfish, sinful, flesh nature and rejoice in the freedom of following the new spirit nature—a spirit of goodness and holiness. We will never receive the power to overcome sin unless by His Spirit we accept forgiveness. Self-effort, self-confidence and self-pride will never attain anything close to what the living Spirit of God has for our lives.

Consider what the psalmist said:

> "If You, Lord, should mark iniquities, O Lord, who could stand? But there is forgiveness with You, that You may be feared" (Psalms 130:3-4).

Self-effort, self-confidence and self-pride will never attain anything close to what the living Spirit of God has for our lives.

This is not the same fear as in 1 John 4:18 above, a fear based on "What if God wants to punish me?" Instead, Psalms 130:4 is a fear based on respect and reverent admiration which says, "What if God prefers to heal and deliver me rather than punish me?" Wouldn't that be awesome? This forgiveness and freedom will work in you with a manifestation of God's power which will be seen by many. They will see Jesus represented by your actions, attitudes and activities.

Reflections

1. Evaluate your thoughts on forgiveness. Do you forgive others? Do you receive forgiveness well? Are you able to forgive yourself?

   _____

   _____

   _____

2. What are you truly and deeply afraid of in your life?

   _____

   _____

   _____

3. Which actions, attitudes and activities are your top priorities which you would be willing to ask a loving God to change in you?

   _____

   _____

   _____

CHAPTER 6

FREE WILL

*"But I say, walk by the Spirit, and you will
not carry out the desire of the flesh. For the
flesh sets its desire against the Spirit, and
the Spirit against the flesh; for these are in
opposition to one another, so that you may
not do the things that you please."*
(Galatians 5:16-17)

Life is a complex series of choices and results.
We learn from experiencing both the pleasing
and not so pleasing results of our choices. But
we also have strong opinions of how life is
"supposed to be." These opinions will often
conflict with the way life is.

Because of this, we can be reluctant to accept
our lives the way they truly are. This creates
a quagmire of consequences which is further
complicated by our free will.

The Lord has given us a free
will, meaning we have the power
of choice. He has done this so
we may decide whether our own
way is best, or His way is best.
But what do we choose and what
will we base our choices on? And
furthermore, what predictable

*The Lord
has given us
a free will,
meaning
we have the
power of
choice.*

and unpredictable results will we get from our many choices?

There seems to be a running pattern in our minds. My preferences-driven will is like a filter which weighs out what I accept or reject in my mind. At the point we come to the Lord, our mind and will has been well trained by this world based on our experiences, our knowledge and our interpretations of how the world works ... or should work. This is actually our worldly, or "fleshly," mind. It is always clamoring for our attention with a thousand and one "urgent" things to consider. But then we hear about the promise of a transformed life.

> *"And do not be conformed to this world, but be transformed by the renewing of your mind, so that you may prove what the will of God is, that which is good and acceptable and perfect"* (Romans 12:2).

It is the Spirit of God, which is birthed within you when you invite Him into your heart, which starts this transformation process. But you still have a free will. You may continue to choose your well-trained clamoring, carnal and confusing ways or you may allow yourself to be transformed.

> *"For those who are according to the flesh set their minds on the things of the flesh, but those who are according to the Spirit, the things of the Spirit. For the mind set on the flesh is death, but the mind set on the Spirit is life and peace, because the mind*

set on the flesh is hostile toward God; for it does not subject itself to the law of God, for it is not even able to do so, and those who are in the flesh cannot please God" (Romans 8:5-8).

Our soul longs for our mind to be in quiet communion with God.

"And the peace of God, which surpasses all comprehension, will guard your hearts and minds in Christ Jesus" (Philippians 4:7).

Honestly, isn't real peace a deep, inner longing of our soul? The soul is where we truly communicate with God and the Holy Spirit. It is where we receive the power to live life and life more abundantly. It is where "deep calls to deep" (Psalms 42:7a).

Reflections

1. List examples of the results of your better and your poorer choices.

   _____

   _____

   _____

2. Describe what a transformed life might look like for you.

   _____

   _____

   _____

3. Rate yourself in the quantity and quality of peace in your life.

   _____

   _____

   _____

CHAPTER 7

WHAT ABOUT OUR THOUGHT LIFE?

*Let the wicked forsake his way and the
unrighteous man his thoughts;
and let him return to the Lord, and He will
have compassion on him, and to our God,
for He will abundantly pardon.*
(Isaiah 55:7)

It has often been said that the battlefield is in the mind. Most of us just let our minds wander to a variety of thoughts or subjects. With our mind we ponder the things of life. We dwell on people, current events or circumstances. With our mind we weigh both great and small decisions. We even put our minds on worldly "autopilot" when we release our minds to whatever we are watching, whether it is a screen or something related to the world around us.

Let's look at a quote which has been accredited to Lao Tzu, an ancient Chinese philosopher. This parallels several Christian concepts: "Watch your thoughts, they become your words; watch your words, they become your actions; watch your actions, they become your habits; watch your habits, they become your character; watch your character, it becomes your destiny." This definitely illustrates the importance of disciplining your mind and is worth consideration and application to our lives.

There are multiple verses in the Bible which tell us about what to dwell on, what to think about and even what not to think about. One is a summary statement found toward the end of the book of Philippians:

> *"Finally, brethren, whatever is true, whatever is honorable, whatever is right, whatever is pure, whatever is lovely, whatever is of good repute, if there is any excellence and if anything worthy of praise, dwell on these things. The things you have learned and received and heard and seen in me, practice these things, and the God of peace will be with you"* (Philippians 4:8-9).

We need the peace of God with us to be able to represent Him well. Paul the Apostle warns us this way:

> *"For though we live in the world, we do not wage war as the world does. The weapons we fight with are not the weapons of the world. On the contrary, they have divine power to demolish strongholds. We demolish arguments and every pretension that sets itself up against the knowledge of God, and we take captive every thought to make it obedient to Christ"* (2 Corinthians 10:3-5, NIV).

Godly thoughts create Godly words, actions, habits, character and destiny. The other thoughts are what I like to call "stinkin' thinkin'." They lead us in all sorts of enemy inspired paths which will lead us away from the wonderful life God has for us.

Godly thoughts create Godly words, actions, habits, character and destiny.

Our key verse above implies the wicked should stop doing wickedness and those who are righteous should stop thinking wickedness. If you wish to be righteous in God's eyes, seriously consider our key verse above as you evaluate your thought life. In addition, please do not confuse self-righteousness with the righteousness of God. The self-righteous, if they will admit it, have a thought life which is full of prideful self-confidence and is extremely displeasing to God. Also, consider this: God hears your thought life out loud and still loves you. God guides us and will empower us to a better thought life. It is part of the process of our sanctification.

Reflections

1. Describe why your own thought life is or isn't important.

   _____

   _____

   _____

2. Give a few personal examples of "stinkin' thinkin'."

   _____

   _____

   _____

3. What steps will you consider taking as you consider the concept that God hears your thought life out loud?

   _____

   _____

   _____

CHAPTER 8

BEING OR DOING?

The world is passing away,
and also its lusts; but the one who
does the will of God lives forever.
(1 John 2:17)

The account of Biblical, New Testament salvation began with John's baptism of repentance.

"John the Baptist appeared in the wilderness preaching a baptism of repentance for the forgiveness of sins" (Mark 1:4).

Until you admit your need for real repentance, or rather a need for salvation from whatever messes up your life, there is not much hope for real inward change. There is only self-effort. But when the God of the universe steps in with His forgiveness and grace a whole new world opens up.

"How blessed is he whose transgression is forgiven, whose sin is covered!"
(Psalms 32:1)

The joy and new life that forgiveness creates is not only the miracle of a massive burden lifted, but also a mammoth sense of gratitude. How are we to express this great gratitude for receiving God's salvation? The natural tendency is to want to do something for the one we owe this enormous debt of gratitude. This is the beginning of the quest for the will of God in our lives. Our key verse tells us the world is passing away, but if we want eternal life, we must do the will of God. Therefore, to not know and, more importantly, to not do the will of God keeps us from eternal life.

Contrary to the world, the working out of your salvation involves what God wants you to be for Him first and then what He wants you to do for Him second. The doing is the overflow of being. An example would be woodworking. If you want to do woodworking well, you have to be a trained woodworker. Being a woodworker requires practice to develop your skills. There is a general skill set required for woodworking which is followed by the development of your specialty. Being a Christian requires practice to develop your skills. There is a general skill set required for understanding and practicing Christianity. With discipline your Christian specialty will develop.

> *The doing is the overflow of being.*

What resources and tools do we have to grow our general Christian skill set? Fellowship with mature believers is necessary to see an example of Christianity in action. We also learn God's ways by reading and studying His written Word. It is the language God speaks. God's Spirit breathes new life in us as we listen to Him speak. The Holy Spirit holds the power to transform our lives and is the translator of God's Word. Prayer and faith are vital. Prayer is a willful separation from the noise of the world so we may be still and listen. We also may make our requests known to God. The best comes as we learn to use the tools of grace, love and mercy. God develops the work of our specialty as we find the joy of doing something which is greater than ourselves—a work empowered by God which has eternal significance. That day, when we see Him face to face, we will not fear punishment. We will thank Him for what we have become and thank Him for what we have done by following His desires for our life.

Reflections

1. Survey your life and identify a few changes in yourself you would like to be empowered to accomplish.

_____

_____

_____

2. What knowledge or skills would be required to accomplish these changes?

_____

_____

_____

3. Evaluate where you believe the knowledge and skills may be found to accomplish these changes.

_____

_____

_____

CHAPTER 9

SUFFERING

That I may know Him and the power of His resurrection and the fellowship of His sufferings, being conformed to His death; in order that I may attain to the resurrection from the dead.
(Philippians 3:10-11)

Is the power of His resurrection a concept we understand or is it a truth which we live? The power of His resurrection is the power which overcomes the corruption of the flesh. This corruption pushes us to the grave through the devil and his world system. Resurrection power is a life-giving power. It is a power which changes who we are.

"But you are a chosen race, a royal priesthood, a holy nation, a people for God's own possession, so that you may proclaim the excellencies of Him who has called you out of darkness into His marvelous light"
(1 Peter 2:9).

The Apostle Paul gives us this caution:

"And do not be conformed to this world, but be transformed by the renewing of your mind, so that you may prove what the will of God is, that which is good and acceptable and perfect" (Romans 12:2).

The power of His resurrection is overcoming power, transforming power ... the power to live a new life.

We hear the power of His resurrection preached regularly, but we hear very little preached about the fellowship of His suffering. We generally don't like the concept of suffering. Jesus, our example, suffered tremendously. The apostles suffered:

> *"They took his [Gamaliel's] advice; and after calling the apostles in, they flogged them and ordered them not to speak in the name of Jesus, and then released them. So they went on their way from the presence of the Council, rejoicing that they had been considered worthy to suffer shame for His name. And every day, in the temple and from house to house, they kept right on teaching and preaching Jesus as the Christ"* (Acts 5:40-42).

Most of my suffering has been the result my stiff-necked, rebellious, ungodly attitudes and choices. Do not be discouraged in your hardships. They are the training grounds to develop you into being an overcomer. Standing for Christ to the point of persecution is a growth process. God calls and equips some to grow to this level of maturity in Christ.

Most of my suffering has been the result my stiff-necked, rebellious, ungodly attitudes and choices.

"Do not be surprised, my brothers and sisters, if the world hates you"
(1 John 3:13, NIV).

In today's world, many Christians fear to even speak the name of Jesus in their daily interactions with people. The love of God is essential for us to persevere and overcome.

"Who will separate us from the love of Christ? Will tribulation, or distress, or persecution, or famine, or nakedness, or danger, or sword?" (Romans 8:35)

Please understand we have to wake up as the people of God in order to demonstrate the power of God and win people to the living, almighty God. What then can we say? If our suffering is not because of our stand for Him, then maybe we stand more for self than for Him. Maybe we have not yet learned the power of abiding in Him: the power which enables us to stand up, speak up and represent Christ well to those around us.

Reflections

1. List a few areas of your life where God's power might help you.

   _____

   _____

   _____

2. Suffering is a part of life. What are your thoughts and feelings concerning undeserved suffering?

   _____

   _____

   _____

3. Describe the suffering that may accompany the abundant life promised by God?

   _____

   _____

   _____

CHAPTER 10

TURNING

Therefore I, the prisoner of the Lord,
implore you to walk in a manner
worthy of the calling with
which you have been called.
(Ephesians 4:1)

There seems to be an end-times scheme to pull believers away from the living God. It is characterized by the busyness of rapid-fire images, media, news, activities, entertainment and the like. These create a giant vacuum force pulling us away from God, our creator, sustainer, protector, provider, confidant and friend. We seem to fellowship with the world more than we fellowship with His truth and His presence. The world's distractions result in a lack of true peace from our Prince of Peace.

> *"Do not love the world nor the things in the world. If anyone loves the world, the love of the Father is not in him"* (1 John 2:15).

There is an Old Testament truth which is a key to finding the peace of God and making God truly bigger in our hearts than the distractions and trials of the world.

> *"If I shut up the heavens so that there is no rain, or if I command the locust to devour*

the land, or if I send pestilence among My people, and My people who are called by My name humble themselves and pray and seek My face and turn from their wicked ways, then I will hear from heaven, will forgive their sin and will heal their land" (2 Chronicles 7:13-14).

Humbling ourselves and praying is our given starting point. Do we have ears to hear this? "Seek My face" not just His hand (His blessings). To seek His face means to seek His character, His love, His desire and His will. These are required first if we are to experience the benefits of His hand.

Often, I have heard people quote this verse and leave out "turn from their wicked ways." If we are not very careful, our form of Godliness will include a dependency on a carnal mind and a self-dependency which can either justify or blind us to our "wicked ways."

When we skip over this turning from our wicked ways, we have already made up our mind nothing is wicked enough in our ways to hinder God's forgiveness and healing. Either that or we have decided because of grace, God is OK with our wickedness. We sometimes label these as our weaknesses or inappropriate choices. We must not presume on an absolute grace which excuses wickedness found in our lives.

> *We must not presume on an absolute grace which excuses wickedness found in our lives.*

"What shall we say then? Are we to continue in sin so that grace may increase? May it never be! How shall we who died to sin still live in it?" (Romans 6:1-2)

God has never been tolerant of wickedness, but He does rejoice in our repentance from wickedness which activates His power to turn us away from evil.

God uses and blesses those who are quick to confess evil and have developed the practice of righteous thoughts, attitudes and actions. But, we must seek His face.

"He who believes in Me, as the Scripture said, 'From his innermost being will flow rivers of living water'" (John 7:38).

Those living waters will be life and growth to those around us. We may then be a part of healing our land! God is always calling us to admit and agree with Him about the condition of the inside of our cup, not to condemn us, but because He wants to clean us, use us and empower us for the healing of ourselves and then the healing our land. Do not let this broken world distract you from God's plan for healing and restoration.

Reflections

1. Evaluate and list a few of the activities in your life which lead you away from the life you long to have.

    _____

    _____

    _____

2. Considering the conditions of the world, which aspects of the 2 Chronicles 7:13-14 progression to healing of the land do you neglect?

    _____

    _____

    _____

3. How would sincerely believing God's desire to bless you and heal your "land" change your life?

    _____

    _____

    _____

CHAPTER 11

SOMETHING IS WRONG

Cease from anger and forsake wrath; do not fret; it leads only to evildoing. For evildoers will be cut off, but those who wait for the Lord, they will inherit the land.
(Psalms 37:8-9)

Lord, please deliver us from the deep, inner core notion that "something" is wrong. This attitude is a filter through which many of our thoughts and emotions seem to flow. The source of this crippling attitude sometimes comes from a life history of unresolved personal issues or even denied brokenness. You know, those areas of brokenness that are just never talked about or admitted. Examples include a past with the many varieties of abuses which cripple our families and our lives. It could even be "lesser" crippling affects, such as habits of unhealthy conflict resolution, fits of rage or even unrealistic expectations.

All of these contribute to a pervasive inner sense that something or someone is wrong. This often results in a judgmental attitude and a crippling lack of joy. It translates into an attitude of people being wrong and a hidden personal need to be "right." It becomes a lack of grace and a lack of humility. It is the carrying of too many burdens.

It translates to an inability to rest in Him, submit to Him, and trust Him. Maybe we need to identify what is actually "wrong" by first searching for the truth inside of ourselves?

The greater question is not what is wrong, but what is right or, more accurately, WHO is right? The Lord, God and King Almighty is right and righteous in every single detail. He is a holy, perfect God who is intimately interested in every aspect of your life and all the struggles of this world.

If you don't believe this, read The Book. He has a character development and life transforming plan second to none. It starts with never forgetting and always admitting we have been wrong in so many ways.

> *"But now apart from the Law, the righteousness of God has been manifested, being witnessed by the Law and the Prophets, even the righteousness of God through faith in Jesus Christ for all those who believe; for there is no distinction; for all have sinned and fall short of the glory of God"* (Romans 3:21-23).

God's truth humbles us, but His intent is never to humiliate us. He transforms us as we put on His righteousness and turn away from the illusion of our own righteousness. The good news is:

God's truth humbles us, but His intent is never to humiliate us.

"What then shall we say to these things? If God is for us, who is against us?" (Romans 8:31)

We must never forget that He alone is right and He alone can and will make all things right in His timing. So do not fret over the evil around you. Cooperate with the Lord to remove the evil from within you.

"Mark the blameless man, and behold the upright; for the man of peace will have a posterity. But transgressors will be altogether destroyed; the posterity of the wicked will be cut off" (Psalms 37:37-38).

Reflections

1. Describe a few of the situations or people which are not "right" in your life.

_____

_____

_____

2. Analyze and comment on your own need to be right and your own evaluation of what is wrong in the world around you.

_____

_____

_____

3. What advantages could there be in a plan to humble yourself?

_____

_____

_____

CHAPTER 12

MY OWN UNDERSTANDING

Because the carnal mind is enmity against God: for it is not subject to the law of God, neither indeed can be.
(Romans 8:7, KJV)

Today, I fired my flesh-natured, carnal mind. Today, I confessed and agreed with God that my own understanding is warped and no good.

"Trust in the Lord with all your heart and do not lean on your own understanding. In all your ways acknowledge Him, and He will make your paths straight. Do not be wise in your own eyes; fear the Lord and turn away from evil. It will be healing to your body and refreshment to your bones" (Proverbs 3:5-8).

I need healing and refreshment! How about you? Today I agreed with God that He has the ultimate right to be heard in any circumstance. My thoughts and feelings do not have the ultimate say.

"The One forming light and creating darkness, causing well-being and creating calamity; I am the Lord who does all these. Drip down, O heavens, from above. And let the clouds pour down righteousness; let the

earth open up and salvation bear fruit. And righteousness spring up with it. I, the Lord, have created it. Woe to the one who quarrels with his Maker—an earthenware vessel among the vessels of earth! Will the clay say to the potter, 'What are you doing?' Or the thing you are making say, 'He has no hands?'" (Isaiah 45:7-9)

Why question God? Why not instead find the truly satisfying answers He provides by His Holy Spirit which opens His Word to your heart?

Today is a new day. I realize that only He has what it takes for me to live my life well. And there is more good news: He is more than willing to patiently come along side and guide me!

Oh seekers, give up on your own understanding and efforts. Agree with God and watch Him move powerfully! Oh, how I long for the Spirit to be the one who has the first and final say! The flesh-natured and worldly side of my mind is like a broken, static-filled radio which is tuned to a hundred stations at the same time. It has no peace; it cannot have peace.

"For the mind set on the flesh is death, but the mind set on the Spirit is life and peace" (Romans 8:6).

The carnal side of my mind is corrupt and unqualified to lead. It soils my soul like pollution in water. The Holy Spirit is life to my soul

The Holy Spirit is life to my soul and the renewal of my mind.

and the renewal of my mind.

Oh LORD, save and cleanse my soul so I may dwell in Your presence and live life as You intended it to be. I choose to live in respectful awe of You so I may have You as my defender to guard and guide me.

"The angel of the Lord encamps around those who fear Him, and rescues them. O taste and see that the Lord is good; how blessed is the man who takes refuge in Him!" (Psalms 34:7-8)

Reflections

1. Analyze at least one way your mind "plays tricks" on you which leads you to unexpected or unpleasant results.

   _____

   _____

   _____

2. Explain what disturbs you about the concept of giving up on self and instead submitting fully to an all-loving, all-knowing, all-powerful God. (This does not violate your free will. It gives you the option to freely choose God's ways instead of the ways of the world.)

   _____

   _____

   _____

3. What does it look like or what would it look like in your life to "taste and see that the Lord is good"?

   _____

   _____

   _____

CHAPTER 13

GUILT AND SHAME

*Instead of your shame you will have a
double portion, and instead of humiliation
they will shout for joy over their portion.
Therefore they will possess a
double portion in their land,
everlasting joy will be theirs.*
(Isaiah 61:7)

There is no guilt or shame in agreeing with God concerning our areas of unbelief, only the opportunity for abiding in Him and His protection.

"Take care, brethren, that there not be in any one of you an evil, unbelieving heart that falls away from the living God" (Hebrews 3:12).

There is no guilt or shame in a believer who agrees with God about their sin, only an opportunity for deliverance.

"But encourage one another day after day, as long as it is still called 'Today' so that none of you will be hardened by the deceitfulness of sin" (Hebrews 3:13).

"Today if you hear His voice, do not harden your hearts." (Hebrews 3:15a)

There is no guilt or shame in agreeing with God regarding

our prideful denial of our need for deep, inner cleansing, only the opportunity for an eternally significant life.

"For we have become partakers of Christ, if we hold fast the beginning of our assurance firm until the end, while it is said, 'Today if you hear His voice, do not harden your hearts, as when they provoked Me.'" (Hebrews 3:14-15)

For a more complete application and understanding, spend some time reflecting on Hebrews 3:16-4:7.

CHAPTER 14

GRUMBLING AND COMPLAINING

*Enter His gates with thanksgiving
and His courts with praise.
Give thanks to Him, bless His name.
(Psalms 100:4)*

Thanksgiving allows us to be in God's "front yard." We have passed through His gate. We can certainly grasp and understand thanksgiving. There is something about being born into the Spirit of God that produces thankfulness deep within us. Thanksgiving is one of our spirit man's banners.

Unfortunately, we often forget to be thankful. Difficult times easily cause us to forget to be thankful. Our natural man wants to focus on what is wrong but our spirit man knows what or, more correctly, who is right and for this we should be thankful. We serve a right, just, trustworthy, all-powerful God who loves us. He wants to encourage us, protect us and defend us.

A loving God never ceases to arrange or rearrange circumstances to teach us how we can apply what we "know." However, our grumbling and complaining is like questioning the God of all circumstances: "Are you sure you know what You are doing?" Please be careful to remember what happens to grumblers and complainers:

> *"Then they despised the pleasant land; they did not believe in His word, but grumbled in their tents; they did not listen to the voice of the Lord. Therefore He swore to them that He would cast them down in the wilderness"* (Psalms 106:24-26).

The long and the short of it is this: People do not grumble and complain because of circumstances, they grumble and complain because that is who they are—grumblers and complainers. A grumbling and complaining heart will not pass through His gates, much less enter into His courts.

> **A grumbling and complaining heart will not pass through His gates, much less enter into His courts.**

> *"The steadfast of mind You will keep in perfect peace, because he trusts in You. Trust in the Lord forever, for in God the Lord, we have an everlasting Rock"* (Isaiah 26:3-4).

Reflections

1. Identify and list a few reasons why you find it hard to trust. It may be a person or circumstance which hurts you deeply.

   _____

   _____

   _____

2. God wants you to trust Him. The enemy, satan, wants you to "trust" him. Evaluate who you would rather or rather not place your trust in and consider why.

   _____

   _____

   _____

3. Give your own analysis of grumbling and complaining concerning what it does and does not accomplish.

   _____

   _____

   _____

CHAPTER 15

WE CHANGE BEFORE THINGS CHANGE

*Glory in His holy name; let the heart
of those who seek the Lord be glad.
Seek the Lord and His strength;
seek His face continually.*
(Psalms 105:3-4)

We all have our wish list for God. You know, the concerns we wish He would fix, make better or put right. For example, heal my hurts and pains, fix my finances and maybe even change another person. Or how about make me happy? God wants to do all these for us, but sometimes it isn't done as we expect. He may fix our aches and pains by taking us home to heaven. Or, He may fix them by asking us to take better care of ourselves in our diet and physical activity. He may fix our finances by providing us with a second job. Or, He may fix our finances through our generous giving and being careful how we spend what is left. He may, instead of changing that other person, change your attitude toward that person. So often we want to see the circumstances around us change, but God wants to see change inside of us.

In those times when I am at the end of my rope crying out to God for an outside change, He usually provides the conviction and power for me to make a change inside. First, we change and that changes our views on what surrounds us. An example of this process is salvation. He brings us from death to life and, behold, all things become new. If we would fully cooperate with Him on the inside changes, He will magnificently rearrange the outside situations ... in time. After all, He is the God of all circumstances. He fixes broken things and we all have our broken places. But, oh, how He makes use of those who are mended in this broken world.

What about the last item on our previously mentioned wish list? How will He make us happy? Not by changing circumstances, but by changing our attitude toward circumstances. If we focus on the broken world, we will be discouraged (unhappy), but when we focus on Him who is perfect, we will be encouraged (happier).

> *"The Lord is my strength and my shield; my heart trusts in Him, and I am helped; therefore my heart exults [triumphs], and with my song I shall thank Him"* (Psalms 28:7).

Seek and trust Him. The overflow of peace and contentment found in Him is joy, which is often accompanied by the feeling of happiness. Joy is a state of heart and mind. Happiness is a pleasurable feeling we love to experience. Lord, help us to receive the fullness of joy which will not only make us happy, but give us the added valuable benefit of contentment.

When we seek His face and not His hand, He will bring honor and glory to His name through the living testimony which results from seeking Him. He will not honor and glorify a list of what we want Him to do. God-sized results will come when we align our list with His list of what He wants us to become and do. It is in His will that we find our true happiness.

> *It is in His will that we find our true happiness.*

Reflections

1. List a few ways God may creatively answer some of the requests on your "wish" list.

   _____

   _____

   _____

2. Are you joyful (filled with joy)? Evaluate why or why not.

   _____

   _____

   _____

3. What God-sized results can you expect from seeking His face instead of His hand?

   _____

   _____

   _____

CHAPTER 16

OPINIONS CAUSE ISSUES

*Finally, brethren, whatever is true,
whatever is honorable, whatever is right,
whatever is pure, whatever is lovely,
whatever is of good repute, if there is any
excellence and if anything worthy of praise,
dwell on these things.*
(Philippians 4:8)

I am continuing to grow in my distaste for opinions. Opinions trigger issues; truth settles issues. By the way, the Truth is a person—

"Jesus said to him, 'I am the way, and the truth, and the life'" (John 14:6a).

The truth is also found in God's word:

"Sanctify them in the truth; Your word is truth" (John 17:17).

Opinions, especially negative opinions, are usually judgmental and God has never invited us to sit on His judgment seat. We are not qualified.

"Do not judge so that you will not be judged" (Matthew 7:1).

Jesus repeatedly proclaimed and practiced truth, grace, mercy and love. Jesus' judgments were based on a correctly applied Law of God. The ones Jesus was critical of were those who misrepresented God and who led people astray. So many are doing the same today.

>*"Let not many of you become teachers, my brethren, knowing that as such we will incur a stricter judgment"* (James 3:1).

Humor me and follow the typical progression of opinions and how they create issues in our lives and with other people:

1. Someone finds the actions of another person or institution to be offensive or in violation of their personal world view.

2. They form an opinion, often conflicting, with very little information or knowledge of all the surrounding conditions.

3. Additional evidence is gathered or invented to support the opinion.

4. This opinion is then exalted into a state of truth in that person's eyes.

5. Then they go and find people who agree with the opinion and thus bolster the exaltation of their opinion to the level of truth.

6. Then they become aggravated with and separated from anyone who disagrees with their opinion because, in their view, it is the truth.

As these steps progress, they move us farther and farther away from truth, grace, mercy and love. Consider these steps in the divisions among our churches, denominations and even Christianity as a whole.

Even more disturbing is seeing this process in our social interactions, social media, news and politics. These, coupled with the internet, are a never-ending stream of opinions, with very little truth. Most disturbing, is seeing the above progression in our marriages and families.

Exalting opinions to the level of truth causes the Spirit of Truth to depart. Exalting opinions causes division, dissension and a root of bitterness. Opinion-oriented people usually have a sour judgmental attitude and lack of peace. Christ-oriented, or rather truth-oriented, people trust God and His Word to be the Judge in all things, especially themselves.

> *Exalting opinions to the level of truth causes the Spirit of Truth to depart.*

Christ-oriented people are inclined to concern themselves more with loving than judging. Self-oriented people are inclined to concern themselves more with judging than loving. Our much-deserved judgment does not draw us to God. His grace, mercy, love and forgiveness draw us to Him. We should go and do the same.

> *"You therefore, my son, be strong in the grace that is in Christ Jesus"* (2 Timothy 2:1).

> *"For judgment will be merciless to one who has shown no mercy; mercy triumphs over judgment"* (James 2:13).

God both holds and withholds judgment.

Reflections

1. Speculate on why opinions seem to be such a point of focus today.

   _____

   _____

   _____

2. How much of your life is complicated by conflicting opinions, primarily with family, but also with others?

   _____

   _____

   _____

3. Describe what your life would become with fewer opinions and more truth.

   _____

   _____

   _____

CHAPTER 17

JUDGMENT

Do nothing from selfishness or empty conceit, but with humility of mind regard one another as more important than yourselves ... Have this attitude in yourselves which was also in Christ Jesus.
(Philippians 2:3, 5)

The only thing we can control is our own attitude. Maintaining a positive, encouraging, godly attitude takes discipline, training and the Spirit of Truth dwelling within us. The only thing a negative, condemning attitude will do is snatch us out of fellowship with the Lord God Almighty.

"For in the way you judge, you will be judged; and by your standard of measure, it will be measured to you. Why do you look at the speck that is in your brother's eye, but do not notice the log that is in your own eye?"
(Matthew 7:2-3)

I'm sure all of us would much rather fellowship with the God of the universe than face His judgment as mentioned in the previous verse. What about the "speck" and the "log" analogy Jesus shared? The speck represents the shortcomings or sins of others.

"You hypocrite, first take the log out of your own eye, and then you will see clearly to

take the speck out of your brother's eye" (Matthew 7:5).

The log in our eye is not our own sin; otherwise, it would also be called a speck. The log represents how we sit in the judgment seat with our condescending, negative opinions of those whom God loves. We are not qualified nor invited to occupy the judgment seat.

"The Lord reigns forever; he has estalished his throne for judgment" (Psalms 9:7, NIV).

He is the judge. This "log" of sitting on the judgment seat sows discord and strife whenever our self-nature brings an inappropriate attitude to a person or group. We did not die for other people's sin; Christ died for ours! Therefore, He has the right to judge and is the only one who can judge rightly. We are commanded to love.

"How blessed is the man who does not walk in the counsel of the wicked, nor stand in the path of sinners, nor sit in the seat of scoffers!" (Psalms 1:1)

When we are judgmental, we walk in pride and sit in the seat of scoffers. Scoffing is the manifestation of contempt by insulting words or actions and it is rooted in a sense of superiority. True believers humble themselves under the love of God and He saves us to liberty and obedience. This liberty allows us to be reconciled to God and others. He saves us with truth—the truth about ourselves and the truth about Him. We are to walk in His Spirit of Truth. Again, this takes discipline, training and, most of all, the leadership of the Holy Spirit of God. We cannot do this in our own strength, otherwise we could save ourselves. We should know this: loving others with grace and mercy, giving thanks in everything and trusting God results in the exchange of stress

He saves us with truth—the truth about ourselves and the truth about Him.

and anxiety for His great peace. This peace is the sweet aroma of Christ to others and it transcends our understanding.

Leave all judgment to Him.

"Shall not the Judge of all the Earth do right?" (Genesis 18:25c, KJV)

In the area of judgment, concern yourself only with the areas of your life where He could judge you. This requires a humbling of ourselves, which will produce thanksgiving to God and spiritual growth. It will also equip us to carry out the greatest commandment:

"And He said to him, 'You shall love the Lord your God with all your heart, and with all your soul, and with all your mind.' This is the great and foremost commandment. The second is like it, 'You shall love your neighbor as yourself'" (Matthew 22:37-39).

Be sure your standards of grace, mercy and love are offered to others more than you offer them to yourself.

Reflections

1. List some examples of gracious and merciful correction you have offered to others.

   _____

   _____

   _____

2. Ask the Lord's help and honestly describe yourself concerning the quality of your attitude and judgments toward those around you.

   _____

   _____

   _____

3. Describe why it may be necessary to receive the Lord's love for yourself in order to show His love to others?

   _____

   _____

   _____

CHAPTER 18

TO LOVE OR TO ACCUSE?

"A new commandment I give to you, that you love one another, even as I have loved you, that you also love one another. By this all men will know that you are My disciples, if you have love for one another."
(John 13:34-35)

We are most like Christ when we love other people, even more so when we are also aware of their faults. Jesus is aware of all our faults and He loves us anyway. This is called GRACE— God's Riches At Christ's Expense. Loving people is difficult in our own strength.

People are messy. We are messy. In fact, some people are what you might call "grace meters." When they get in our face, or anyone else's face, they measure just how much grace we have. With God, it is possible to love them anyway. That is one way people will know we are disciples of Christ—by the way we love others.

On the other hand, we move into the enemy's camp when we accuse others of their faults.

"For the accuser of our brethren has been thrown down, he who accuses them before our God day and night" (Revelation 12:10b).

Let us not align ourselves with the enemy's accusing behavior.

Many of us turn a blind eye to our own sins, faults and cravings, thus giving ourselves more grace than we ever give anyone else. If we do this, we misuse God's grace and treat His grace as a "get-out-of-jail-free card." The problem is we turn around and walk back into the jail by continuing self-crippling, unrighteous behaviors. It is Christ's love which sets you free.

> *"It was for freedom that Christ set us free; therefore keep standing firm and do not be subject again to a yoke of slavery"*
> (Galatians 5:1).

Do not be enslaved to unrighteousness and do not be crippled by prideful self-righteousness. Put on the humble righteousness of Christ by spending time with the Lord. Through His love He will gently, without condemnation, provide conviction along with the desire and ability to move away from bad behavior. Conviction comes from the Lord and is wrapped in freedom. Condemnation comes from satan and is wrapped in hopelessness.

Conviction comes from the Lord and is wrapped in freedom. Condemnation comes from satan and is wrapped in hopelessness.

This hopeless condemnation prevents you from a healthy love of self which prevents you from loving others. So, how do we grow to love others with the love of Christ? We grow to love others when we spend intimate time with Jesus. We will be led by His Spirit to truly accept His love—that agape love which enables us to truly love others. We will be empowered to choose love instead of choosing to accuse.

What is your heart's desire in all this? Bringing loving encouragement to others brings a smile to your soul and definitely brings a smile to Jesus as He tells the angels: "Look! There is one fulfilling My Great Commandment!"

> "And you shall love the Lord your God with all your heart, and with all your soul, and with all your mind, and with all your strength.' The second is this, 'You shall love your neighbor as yourself.' There is no other commandment greater than these" (Mark 12:30-31).

Spend intimate times with God in Bible study and prayer. Do not mistake the Bible for a book of hard, unreachable standards but a book of change and growth. You will grow to love Him and you will grow to love others.

> "Behold, I say to you, lift up your eyes and look on the fields, that they are white for harvest" (John 4:35b).

It is a harvest of lives whose true, deep and inner longing is to be transformed by the love of God.

Reflections

1. Identify a specific situation where you find it difficult to love someone and speculate how the Lord could change this.

   _____

   _____

   _____

2. In your own words define the difference between conviction and condemnation.

   _____

   _____

   _____

3. List one or more steps the Lord may be encouraging you to take to improve your love for others.

   _____

   _____

   _____

CHAPTER 19

THE DISHONESTY OF DECEPTION

Do not be deceived, God is not mocked;
for whatever a man sows,
this he will also reap.
(Galatians 6:7)

You cannot plant a watermelon seed and hope to get corn. What you plant is what you get. There is disappointment where deception lives. We are deceived when there is a difference between who we think we are and who our words, actions and attitudes say that we are. These words, actions *You cannot plant a watermelon seed and hope to get corn.* and attitudes become pleasing to the Lord when they are driven by the love of His Spirit and the love of His truth working together. His truth with just our own fleshly understanding and agenda will surely malign His good name and bear the rotten fruit of self-righteousness, which is clothed in self and not clothed in Christ.

> *"Let the words of my mouth and the meditation of my heart be acceptable in Your sight, O Lord, my rock and my Redeemer"* (Psalms 19:14).

What does "acceptable in His sight" mean? He sees everything and nothing is hidden. We cannot fool Him, but we surely can fool ourselves and sometimes even others.

The enemy, satan, loves deception because it is rooted in a lie.

"When he lies, he speaks his native language, for he is a liar and the father of lies" (John 8:44c, NIV)

He knows deception cripples our ability to live well. Rest assured, the enemy will do everything he can to render us ineffective for the cause of Christ—to free and rescue souls. Be aware, satan hates all of us and he takes pleasure in destroying people. God loves people. However, satan, with his "ministry" of condemnation, will criticize and remind God (and us, if we listen) of every one of our flaws in hope that God will also judge us as the enemy himself has been judged. This trickery of the enemy makes a mess wherever it is found.

There is no righteousness in the presence of the dishonesty of deception. It prevents us from seeing the truth about ourselves. It prevents us from a healthy view of others and of circumstances. It gives us the continuous, deep, inner feeling something is not right. Something needs fixing. Our dishonesty with ourselves drives us to be manipulative and controlling because we won't admit the problem is inside with our misguided attitudes and beliefs. So, we keep wishing the outside circumstances would change or that we could fix them. This wishing is futile. When we live like this, fellowship with the Lord often feels hollow and empty.

The web of deception entangles and enslaves. On the other hand, God is a God of truth. He wants us to know the truth, think the truth and live the truth!

"But prove yourselves doers of the word, and not merely hearers who delude themselves" (James 1:22).

When we are still and quiet before Him, He will reveal the truth which removes the deception.

"Cease striving and know that I am God" (Psalms 46:10a).

The book of John says:

"And you will know the truth, and the truth will make you free" (John 8:32).

God reveals the truth about Himself and the truth about us.

"God is spirit, and those who worship Him must worship in spirit and truth" (John 4:24).

Consider these truths presented. Sow these truths both inside and outside yourself. Then you will surely reap blessings and a harvest from the Lord.

Reflections

1. Explain why it is good, even though it may be painful, to allow the Lord to reveal the truth about ourselves.

_____

_____

_____

2. Identify at least one deception of the enemy which prevents you from moving forward in God's plan to create a better life for you.

_____

_____

_____

3. Summarize a few of the expected benefits of truth being sown and grown in your own life.

_____

_____

_____

CHAPTER 20

SELF CANNOT BE TRUSTED

*Do not be hasty in word or impulsive
in thought to bring up a matter in the
presence of God. For God is in heaven
and you are on the earth;
therefore let your words be few.*
(Ecclesiastes 5:2)

Have you ever met anybody who talks constantly and seems only interested in what they have to say? These are often self-appointed experts. This talkativeness could be rooted in pride, a deep underlying insecurity or an unmet need for acceptance. Maturing believers are humble enough to listen. Mature believers find their security and acceptance in Christ. Maturing believers have listened and responded to God's Spirit and Word to become quiet, confident and fit ... mended in this broken world.

Our flesh nature is rooted in pride and selfishness. It is deeply insecure and craves to be accepted. The flesh nature does not want us to *"Be still and know that [He is] God"* (Psalms 46:10a, KJV). An active flesh nature stunts or can even prevent spiritual growth in the Lord. This part of our nature

An active flesh nature stunts or can even prevent spiritual growth in the Lord.

rarely stops talking and is attempting to seize God's rightful place of Lordship in our mind and heart with persistent ungodly babbling. This babbling originates from satan and the influences of this broken world. Our self-natured mind seems to think itself qualified to lead in every area. It supposes we want to hear its prideful boastings about its capabilities.

But in reality, this natural side of us falls short as a leader. Our fallen nature is wrapped up in its own desires which are of the world. It is in conflict with our spirit man and God's better way.

"This is what the Lord says—your Redeemer, the Holy One of Israel: 'I am the Lord your God, who teaches you what is best for you, who directs you in the way you should go'" (Isaiah 48:17, NIV).

This is not a disguise to wear, but a truth to live from our deep inner being. Paul tells us concerning our fleshly sin nature:

"Even so consider yourselves to be dead to sin, but alive to God in Christ Jesus" (Romans 6:11).

The Maker, Master, Ruler, Creator and Sustainer of all things is so much more worthy to be listened to and obeyed than the natural, sinful, petty, self-centered, noisy, and know-it-all side of us. Remember, the enemy is satan, who operates though the world and our flesh nature. The evil of the enemy is active when our flesh is leading.

"For the flesh sets its desire against the

Spirit, and the Spirit against the flesh; for these are in opposition to one another, so that you may not do the things that you please" (Galatians 5:17).

God is not pushy, but leads us by a still small voice which thunders in our soul.

Have you ever met anybody who talks constantly and seems only interested in what they have to say? Is this how my prayer life sounds to God?

"He says, 'Be still, and know that I am God'" (Psalms 46:10a, NIV).

Job said:

"I should never have opened my mouth! I've talked too much, way too much. I'm ready to shut up and listen" (Job 40:4-5, MSG).

Reflections

1. Summarize how your own "mended" life would look on the inside of you. (Remember, God wants this and so much more for you because He loves you enough not to leave you the way you are.)

_____

_____

_____

2. What would you consider to be the greatest benefit of listening to the Spirit of Truth more than listening to the spirit of the flesh?

_____

_____

_____

3. How can you develop your "listening" time with God?

_____

_____

_____

CHAPTER 21

FREEDOM

And you will know the truth,
and the truth will make you free.
(John 8:32)

Lord, let me measure myself by Your truth. Let my opinion of myself align with Your righteous and unbiased judgment of me.

"Justice and judgment are the habitation of Thy throne: mercy and truth shall go before Thy face" (Psalms 89:14, KJV).

Truth heals and reveals. Truth is a deep, inner craving.

"Jesus answered, 'I am the way and the truth and the life'" (John 14:6a, NIV).

Also, we read:

"Behold, Thou desirest truth in the inward parts: and in the hidden part Thou shalt make me to know wisdom"
(Psalms 51:6, KJV).

What a wonderful and comforting promise for us as we seek the application of His truth in our life. This promised wisdom makes good use of and applies the truth which transforms us. If you do not apply the truth, it is just knowledge. Discerning the truth gives you understanding.

Applying truth leads to wisdom and the following freedoms of an abundant life:

- **Free from lies and deceptions**:
  "Keep deception and lies far from me, give me neither poverty nor riches; feed me with the food that is my portion" (Proverbs 30:8).

- **Free from bondages**:
  "It was for freedom that Christ set us free; therefore keep standing firm and do not be subject again to a yoke of slavery"
  (Galatians 5:1).

- **Free from worry and anxiety**:
  "Humble yourselves, therefore, under God's mighty hand, that he may lift you up in due time. Cast all your anxiety on Him because He cares for you" (1 Peter 5:6-7, NIV).

- **Free from self-condemnation**:
  "Therefore there is now no condemnation for those who are in Christ Jesus. For the law of the Spirit of life in Christ Jesus has set you free from the law of sin and of death"
  (Romans 8:1-2).

- **Free to be pleasant to everyone**:
  "Be kind to one another, tender-hearted, forgiving each other, just as God in Christ also has forgiven you" (Ephesians 4:32).

- **Free to follow in close fellowship with the Lord**:
  "He who dwells in the shelter of the Most High will abide in the shadow of the Almighty" (Psalms 91:1).

- **Free to receive forgiveness**:
"And he [John the Baptizer] went into all the region around the Jordan, preaching a baptism of repentance for the forgiveness of sins" (Luke 3:3).

- **Free to follow the Spirit**:
"But the fruit of the Spirit is love, joy, peace, patience, kindness, goodness, faithfness, gentleness, self-control; against such things there is no law" (Galatians 5:22-23).

With all these freedoms, we will, without restraint, bear fruit for the Kingdom of God. We gain all of this because we do not follow the slavery to self-defeating bondages, which are the demonstration of our self-nature caused by damaging and inaccurate opinions of God. Instead, we seek, believe and apply God's truth.

With all these freedoms, we will, without restraint, bear fruit for the Kingdom of God.

"Abide in Me, and I in you. As the branch cannot bear fruit of itself unless it abides in the vine, so neither can you unless you abide in Me" (John 15:4).

We must live and enjoy the fruit of a Christ-like attitude. We are to inspect our own fruit and keep the weeds out of our gardens.

Reflections

1. List the three most important freedoms for you in the above list.

   _____

   _____

   _____

2. Compare and contrast what would help you and or what would hinder you from obtaining these freedoms for yourself.

   _____

   _____

   _____

3. Make a personal list of "weeds" which mess up your garden, then take the list to the Lord in prayer.

   _____

   _____

   _____

CHAPTER 22

OVERCOMING THE ENEMY

I have written to you, fathers, because you know Him who has been from the beginning. I have written to you, young men, because you are strong, and the Word of God abides in you, and you have overcome the evil one.
(1 John 2:14)

We are expected to overcome. The messages in the book of the Revelation to the seven churches teach us this. All seven letters to the seven churches have summary statements that include a specific promise to overcomers:

"He who overcomes ..." and a call to hear, *"He who has an ear, let him hear what the Spirit says to the churches"*
(See Revelation 2:7, 11, 17, 26-29; 3:5-6, 12-13, 21-22).

We are expected to "overcome the evil one;" not in our own strength, but in the strength of God as we apply His truth in an abiding relationship with His living Holy Spirit. It is impossible to lead a victorious Christian life unless the Spirit of God is known to us, abiding in us and leading us. Our own strength is actually weakness concerning this overcoming battle against our enemy.

Additionally, it seems that far too many church members are concerned with what the enemy is doing against them, instead what the living Christ has done for them. Just before He gave up His Spirit on the cross, Jesus said, "It is finished!" The battle with the enemy was won at the cross. When we walk in Christ, we walk in victory! But, do we truly believe we have this victory? The world gives us "evidence" not to believe; faith produces evidence to believe.

"But without faith it is impossible to please Him: for he that cometh to God must believe that He is, and that He is a rewarder of them that diligently seek Him" (Hebrews 11:6, KJV).

This faith is not a 'think-so' faith or a 'hope-so' faith, but a 'know-so' faith.

"Now faith is the assurance of things hoped for, the conviction of things not seen" (Hebrews 11:1a).

Please notice, "Now faith is," not faith someday maybe.

"For whatever is born of God overcomes the world; and this is the victory that has overcome the world—our faith" (1 John 5:4).

You see, the enemy, satan, is the god of this world. Please do not have faith in his ability to cripple you. The power of the enemy was the power of sin.

"And even if our gospel is veiled, it is veiled to those who are perishing, in whose case

the god of this world has blinded the minds of the unbelieving so that they will not see the light of the gospel of the glory of Christ, who is the image of God"
(2 Corinthians 4:3-4).

Jesus came to save us from our sins and to enable us to be overcomers. Consider this:

"She will give birth to a Son and you are to give Him the name Jesus, because He will save His people from their sins"
(Matthew 1:21, NIV).

The Hebrew name Jesus means "God is Salvation." Salvation is not just an event. It is an ever-present process for daily overcoming. He leads me away from sin and self more each day as I exercise my free will choice to be led by Him instead of choosing to be pushed by self, satan and the world.

> *Salvation is not just an event. It is an ever-present process for daily overcoming.*

Now, be certain of this: knowing about God is not the same as knowing God. It is troubling to know there is a wide spectrum of "Christians" who not only fail to genuinely know themselves, but also fail to truly know God. Many are sedated with enough churchianity to make them drones in the sleeping, ineffective army of God which says "I am good enough ... God is OK with me staying just as I am." Additionally, many do not realize Christ has won for us the battle between good and evil, the flesh and the Spirit.

"Know ye not, that to whom ye yield yourselves servants to obey, his servants ye are to whom ye obey; whether of sin unto death, or of obedience unto righteousness? But God be thanked, that ye were the servants of sin, but ye have obeyed from the heart that form of doctrine which was delivered you. Being then made free from sin, ye became the servants of righteousness"
(Romans 6:16-18, KJV).

Who will you serve? Self, the flesh nature and satan leading to death or God, Jesus Christ of Nazareth and His Holy Spirit leading to life? We will never be perfect in this life, but Christ has made provision for us to be so much more like Him than we already are. It's an ongoing process of sanctification.

Reflections

1. From the standpoint of conviction from the Lord and not from the standpoint of the condemnation of the enemy, what has this chapter spoken to your heart? (It reveals in me my daily absolute need for God's protection, guidance and growth.)

   _____

   _____

   _____

2. Set aside some time away from the worries and cares of this world to ponder the words of this chapter. Let God be life, healing and deliverance for you.

   _____

   _____

   _____

CHAPTER 23

WHICH KINGDOM?

*Whatever city you enter and they receive
you, eat what is set before you;
and heal those in it who are sick,
and say to them, "The kingdom
of God has come near to you."*
(Luke 10:8-9)

When Pilate demanded to know if Christ was the King of the Jews, *"Jesus answered, 'My kingdom is not of this world. If My kingdom were of this world, then My servants would be fighting so that I would not be handed over to the Jews; but as it is, My kingdom is not of this realm'"* (John 18:36).

There is something "other worldly" about what Jesus did and is doing through His believers who journey in this world. There are two kingdoms— the Kingdom of God and the kingdom of this world. Adam and Eve were to have dominion over the physical kingdom of this world in God's original Eden plan. Instead, they chose rebellion.

The enemy, satan, is familiar with rebellion. That is why he was cast down from heaven (Isaiah 14:12-19, Revelation 12:7-13). The enemy continues to search for and steal free will from any who will give him dominion over their "world" through self-crippling views and behaviors which are in opposition to God's better free will plan. The enemy craves to enslave and control. God is, and always will be, all powerful. He has authority over us and authority over satan. Even so, God respects our freedom to choose. Even when satan tempted Christ, the enemy was seeking dominance over Jesus.

> *"And the devil said to Him, 'I will give You all this domain and its glory; for it has been handed over to me, and I give it to whomever I wish. Therefore if You worship before me, it shall all be Yours'"* (Luke 4:6-7).

The enemy promises us the world; it is all he has to offer.

> *"For what will it profit a man if he gains the whole world and forfeits his soul? Or what will a man give in exchange for his soul?"* (Matthew 16:26)

The enemy does not have authority in God's Kingdom; he only has some authority in this world. In no way does he respect our free will ... he wants to take it from us. In the Bible, I have never found where satan was given authority over man. That would remove our free will to choose, something foundational which God gave us. When we live the ways of this natural world, we experience the things of this world, which include satan's shenanigans as he steals authority over us.

> *"The thief comes only to steal and kill and destroy; I came that they may have life, and have it abundantly"* (John 10:10).

The enemy wants to steal your peace, your joy, your destiny, your family, your victory, your health ... your whole life and soul. He wants your only choice to be sin and him. This satan uses the lures and lies of this world to steal us away from choosing God's better way of living. This is done by convincing us his way and the world's way is best. It is the easiest, but not the best. As David Henry Thoreau said, "The path of least resistance makes both rivers and men crooked." By accepting God's invitation and rejecting satan's temptation we triumph over the world.

By accepting God's invitation and rejecting satan's temptation we triumph over the world.

> *"These things I have spoken unto you, that in Me ye might have peace. In the world ye shall have tribulation: but be of good cheer; I have overcome the world"* (John 16:33, KJV).

In Him you will have peace, calm in the midst of the storm and life under the shelter of the Almighty. God respects our free will and offers us the opportunity to have the confident hope of living in the kingdom of Jesus Christ. Through faith it will come near to you. On the other hand, satan gives us his offer of the kingdom of this world.

> *"But as for me and my house, we will serve the Lord"* (Joshua 24:15c).

Reflections

1. What are your own thoughts about the choice to rebel or the choice to accept God's way of doing things?

   _____

   _____

   _____

2. Search your heart and describe why you can or cannot believe there are two "kingdoms" around us—the kingdom of God and the kingdom of this world.

   _____

   _____

   _____

3. Consider your life and answer the question of how well has it gone for you when you have acted selfishly versus how well it goes when you are considerate of others.

   _____

   _____

   _____

CHAPTER 24

HEARING PROBLEMS

*Do not worry then, Saying, 'What are we
to eat?' or 'What are we to drink?'
or 'What are we to wear for clothing?'
For the Gentiles eagerly seek all these
things; For your heavenly Father knows
that you need all these things. But seek
first His kingdom and His righteousness,
and all these things will be added to you.*
(Matthew 6:31-33)

If we are not careful when we consider all our many wants and needs, we may create a long, anxiety-producing list of "needs" that are the imaginations of a grumbling, complaining and selfish nature. Presenting these surface needs in prayer may even sound like we are questioning God's provision, goodness, sovereignty and wisdom. On the other hand, Paul the Apostle wrote:

> *"And my God will supply all your needs according to His riches in glory in Christ Jesus"* (Philippians 4:19).

Questioning God's provision was one of the behaviors which got the Israelites in trouble after being freed from Egypt's bondage.

"But the Lord said to Moses, 'Put back the

rod of Aaron before the testimony to be
kept as a sign against the rebels, that you
may put an end to their grumblings against
Me, so that they will not die'"
(Numbers 17:10).

Truthfully, our root want and need is the one the Creator placed in us, which is intimate fellowship with Him. This fellowship is accompanied by the peace and provision which He wants to give as stated in our key verse above:

"But seek first His kingdom and His
righteousness, and all these things will be
added to you" (Matthew 6:33).

This life-changing, quality fellowship is found by learning to turn away from self-indulgence, greed and materialism. Instead, we learn the fruitful Joy of practicing obedience by walking in His Spirit's leading!

The other choice is partnership with the wickedness in the world and the leadership of self and satan. Why not submit to the One in charge?

"Submit yourselves, then, to God. Resist the
devil, and he will flee from you. Come near
to God and He will come near to you. Wash
your hands, you sinners, and purify your
hearts, you double-minded" ·
(James 4:7-8, NIV).

God has given everyone the offer of a life of contentment and peace. With this cleansing, God will allow us to become change agents for the suffering people in our "sphere of influence!"

Additionally, He will equip us to be a positive, healing influence on the people and organizations with which we engage. As we grow in Him, God holds us accountable for those with whom we make contact.

> *"But if the watchman sees the sword coming and does not blow the trumpet and the people are not warned, and a sword comes and takes a person from them, he is taken away in his iniquity; but his blood I will require from the watchman's hand"* (Ezekiel 33:6).

The quality, world-changing fellowship and blessed life we long for develops through a walk of obedience.

> *"And all these blessings shall come upon you and overtake you, because you obey the voice of the Lord your God"* (Deuteronomy 28:2, NKJV).

We can't obey Him if we do not hear Him. We can't hear His Spirit if we don't quiet our natural, carnal and worldly mind. We cannot quiet ourselves before Him unless we can discern good from evil, right from wrong ... even in our thoughts. And we cannot do any of the above if we do not know God through a spiritual rebirth.

We can't obey Him if we do not hear Him.

> *"Jesus answered and said to him, 'Truly, truly, I say to you, unless one is born again he cannot see the kingdom of God'"* (John 3:3).

Be warned, there are many spirits that speak, but what God's Spirit speaks is aligned with the principles of the Bible. Therefore, to hear His Spirit you must know His Word. The Bible is the language God speaks as He trains us to receive His abundant blessings.

Reflections

1. What may prevent you from applying the idea of our key verse which states that if you seek God's spiritual ways, He will provide your physical needs?

   _____

   _____

   _____

2. Give examples of the results of obedience and disobedience in your life.

   _____

   _____

   _____

3. Explain the reasons for reluctance toward obedience to God and His plan for your life.

   _____

   _____

   _____

CHAPTER 25

I CAN'T HANDLE IT

But when this perishable will have
put on the imperishable, and this mortal
will have put on immortality, then will
come about the saying that is written,
"Death is swallowed up in victory.
O death, where is your victory?
O death, where is your sting?"
(1 Corinthians 15:54-55)

Most of the words written in this book originated as insights during prayer time. These were written as journal entries in the journey of the desire to become a well-developed, healthy Christian. One day I was pondering this question, "what is the worst thing which could happen to me today?" My first thought was dying. But then I knew dying would be like entering fully into God's presence! When saying to believers "I am looking forward to graduation," there are generally two responses: one is a morbidly-shocked, head-tilted expression, and the other an "Amen!"

If we are fearful of death, we may want to examine the genuineness of our belief in the glory of heaven, or even more than this, our trust in the Lord. Paul wrote:

*"For to me, to live is Christ and **to die is gain**"* (Philippians 1:21, emphasis by the author).

This does not in any way mean that we should seek death (except death to our sin nature) but, instead, we are not fearful of death. It is God who gave us life; therefore, it is God who should determine its end.

> *"Therefore, being always of good courage, and knowing that while we are at home in the body we are absent from the Lord—for we walk by faith, not by sight—we are of good courage, I say, and prefer rather to be absent from the body and to be at home with the Lord. Therefore we also have as our ambition, whether at home or absent, to be pleasing to Him"* (2 Corinthians 5:6-9).

It pleases God when our attitudes and words reflect a complete unswerving trust in Him. In this type of trust we will find rest and peace. Let God lead you to the life He desires for you.

It pleases God when our attitudes and words reflect a complete unswerving trust in Him.

So, if death is not the worst thing which could happen to me today, then what is? Could it possibly be walking in the "strength" of my self-nature, which is basically walking out of fellowship with God? We all have had weary days from leaning on our own understanding and depending on our own strength. As a true believer in Christ, believing in His power and trustworthiness, the very worst way we could spend our time is walking without His guiding and abiding presence and protection. Without this we will stumble and fall into the snares of this world. Oh! But the fruit of the Spirit we will enjoy, as we truly make Him our moment-by-moment Shepherd and King!

But wait, we may rightly ask: "What about the suffering of crushing circumstances or debilitating diseases?" Well, these too would be worst handled away from the fullness and peace found in the abiding fellowship of fully trusting the Lord. None of our suffering and hardship can compare to the rejection and suffering of Christ.

"The steadfast of mind You will keep in perfect peace, because he trusts in You" (Isaiah 26:3).

"But I say, walk by the Spirit, and you will not carry out the desire of the flesh" (Galatians 5:16).

Also note:

"For all who are being led by the Spirit of God, these are sons of God" (Romans 8:14).

This world and all that is in the world is used by the enemy to devastate us (see 1 John 2:15-17). The Lord has done His part to lift us up from this world, into His Kingdom and all the way to heaven.

"For He rescued us from the domain of darkness, and transferred us to the kingdom of His beloved Son" (Colossians 1:13).

Reflections

1. Examine and comment on your own personal feelings about death.

_____

_____

_____

2. Interpret 2 Corinthians 5:6-9 in the first paragraph above and reflect on the most important concept which applies to you.

_____

_____

_____

3. Describe some advantages to living a "heavenly" lifestyle in this broken world.

_____

_____

_____

CHAPTER 26

INSIDE OR OUTSIDE?

And Jesus said unto him, "Go thy way; thy
faith hath made thee whole."
And immediately he received his sight,
and followed Jesus in the way.
(Mark 10:52, KJV)

Were you raised in a family which had hidden struggles that were not talked about or "seen?" The brokenness that no one seems able or willing to admit or mend: addiction, violence, abuse, anger, hurtful words, lack of love or bad attitudes ... you fill in the blanks. Some were awful and you dare not talk about them. Some were hidden but are still present like a cancer to your soul. Some are kept in the secret place of denial. This leaves us growing up with a nagging sense of "something is broken," "something needs fixing." This something gnaws at our soul and we often look for the problem and the solution on the outside.

We know in our quiet moments something is wrong on the inside, but our true, inner self can be a fearful and relatively undiscovered place protected and sustained by pride, fear and habit. We are familiar with what surrounds us more than what is truly in us. It is sad, but others can see our issues better than we can see our own. God knows all our "hidden" issues and loves us anyway. In view of this, He still offers us His marvelous Salvation Plan.

> *"Behold, the Lord has proclaimed to the end of the earth, Say to the daughter of Zion, 'Lo, your salvation comes; Behold His reward is with Him, and His recompense before Him'"* (Isaiah 62:11).

Jesus brings the reward of salvation to us and then begins the refreshing work of salvation in us.

Jesus brings the reward of salvation to us and then begins the refreshing work of salvation in us.

> *"I will lead the blind by ways they have not known, along unfamiliar paths I will guide them; I will turn the darkness into light before them and make the rough places smooth. These are the things I will do; I will not forsake them"* (Isaiah 42:16, NIV).

Consider this: we are very experienced with sensing and observing things on the outside which we consider "not right." But, as our conviction and understanding from God concerning good and evil increase, we may mistakenly overlay our old ways of primarily focusing on what is obviously wrong around us more than focusing on what is wrong in us. This is the breeding ground of self-righteous pride.

We tend to forget when we lay ourselves before the Lord that He fixes our inside condition so we may see more clearly how to respond to the outside conditions and circumstances in a productive way.

If you are someone quick to describe for others what they need to do to solve their problems, or if you are quick to describe how to solve the problems of the world around you, then you are missing God's desired focus. This focus is delivering you from what gets in the way of representing Him well and thus demonstrating to others His transformational power!

He is not pleased when we have an opinionated and judgmental attitude toward people and activities in the world around us. He is perfectly aware of everything. God is more interested in us inviting His work in our hidden inward parts. He then gives us His peace, which tells us, "You don't need to fix anything. I will fix it all." Only then will you have the ability and desire to both truly be at peace and truly love others.

Rest in Him; let Him do the fixing work in you as you share this truth that transforms. The fields are white unto harvest. Isaiah says it this way:

"You have heard; look at all this. And you, will you not declare it? I proclaim to you new things from this time, even hidden things which you have not known" (Isaiah 48:6).

God changes our "world" from the inside out.

Reflections

1. List a few of the internal struggles you would like to see gone from yourself and/or your family.

   _____

   _____

   _____

2. Analyze and consider why it seems so much easier to focus on what is wrong around us than in us.

   _____

   _____

   _____

3. Generally, many believe God will fix everything in the end. List a few struggles God could fix in you that would change the quality of your time between now and "the end."

   _____

   _____

   _____

CHAPTER 27

TRIP HAZARDS

*Do you not know that when you present
yourselves to someone as slaves for
obedience, you are slaves of the one whom
you obey, either of sin resulting in death, or
of obedience resulting in righteousness?*
(Romans 6:16)

Sin and death or Spirit and life ... the verse is pretty clear, isn't it? So why don't we have a firmly applied grasp of this principle? I don't know, but I have hurt myself and others falling over (and over) on these following stumbling blocks. When we operate from self, we are operating in a sin-based framework. When we are being led by the Spirit, we are following an obedient, God-based framework. One clue is this: the flesh pushes to have its own way. God always offers you the choice of His way. Choosing God's way leads to righteousness and life; choosing the way of the flesh leads to wrongdoing and death.

> *"But thanks be to God that though you were slaves of sin, you became obedient from the heart to that form of teaching to which you were committed, and having been freed from sin, you became slaves of righteous-ness"* (Romans 6:17-18).

We must hate being led by the carnal, fleshly mind. Instead, we could learn to love being led by the Holy Spirit while developing the discernment to know the difference. Please, do not mistake ideas based on Bible principles and developed in the rational mind for Biblically-based understanding directed by the Holy Spirit. This leads to the legalism of the Pharisees and self-righteousness, which gives us masked permission to behave in an ungodly way.

Here is another stumbling block. It is a common struggle. We confuse the way we think God wants to accomplish His plans with the way He actually wants to accomplish His plans. We are highly valued by God, but that doesn't mean our plans, based on our own broken understanding, are favored by God. Know this also, God desires to accomplish His work in you, so you can more effectively partner with His work around you. So much dissension and strife has come in the church and in relationships, from well-intentioned people who believe they know how something should get done and any other opinion but theirs is not from "God." We must examine ourselves in this or we may find ourselves supporting satan's position of stirring up strife by trying to play God. This stumbling block is rooted in pride and self-righteousness.

> *"For through the grace given to me I say to everyone among you not to think more highly of himself than he ought to think; but to think so as to have sound judgment,*

as God has allotted to each a measure of faith" (Romans 12:3).

The mindset of "My way is sanctioned by God" violates His Word:

"Do not be wise in your own eyes; fear the Lord and turn away from evil" (Proverbs 3:7).

The Lord detests dissention among the brethren, but He loves unity.

"How good and pleasant it is when God's people live together in unity!" (Psalms 133:1, NIV)

When people turn away from self-centeredness and choose to be led by the Spirit, there will be unity, for He is one Spirit. Opinions often cause issues; truth settles issues. There is only One who is right and righteous.

Opinions often cause issues; truth settles issues.

Lord, help us to know You and listen to You. Lord, help us to not be frustrated by the struggles of life, but instead follow Your Spirit and truth with all our heart, mind, soul and strength. Then, we may accomplish Your purposes in Your way and for Your glory. Lead us to a harvest of souls won for You, which is Your destiny for those who know you.

"The fruit of the righteous is a tree of life, and he who wins souls is wise" (Proverbs 11:30, NKJV).

Reflections

1. What thoughts and feelings rise up in you as you read our key verse above?

   _____

   _____

   _____

2. Fearlessly identify and analyze how the above stumbling blocks may apply to your own life.

   _____

   _____

   _____

3. Describe what area of giftedness you are equipped with which may be used by God to reach souls and reap a harvest. A trusted friend may see this better than you.

   _____

   _____

   _____

PERFECTIONISM

*For all have sinned and fall short
of the glory of God.*
(Romans 3:23)

Seeking perfection is an infection to our soul. It causes us to be discontent with ourselves because we are never quite "good" enough. It is easy then to believe God doesn't love us because we are not good enough. Striving for perfection is a terrible task master. It causes us to be in bondage to performance-based love, performance-based acceptance and performance-based living. This longing to do things perfectly is rooted in legalism. It is a joy killer and the mother of compulsive behaviors.

Consider this: What if we became closer to perfection in leaps and bounds or if we performed our tasks more perfectly for the rest of our life? There would still remain an infinite number of imperfections which God could list against us if He wanted to. Think about a best friend. Do you love and cherish them because they are perfect? No, you cherish them because you are in a relationship where you care for each other. You don't focus on each other's faults. This mutual valuing of the each other is what gives the relationship its richness. It also allows you to compassionately comfort each other when the world and others crush you because of the massive imperfections of this broken world. What does this analogy with friendship suggest about a relationship with a perfect, compassionate, loving and forgiving God? Paul the Apostle wrote:

> *"Not that I have already attained, or am already perfected; but I press on, that I may lay hold of that for which Christ Jesus has also laid hold of me"*
> (Philippians 3:12, NKJV).

We will be perfect in heaven but, meanwhile, God has provided abundantly for every one of us to have healthy, compassionate relationships: first with Him through Jesus Christ and then our other relationships will improve. We can be sure of this: If our relationship with Jesus is not working well, neither will our relationships with others work well. We cause the relationship to suffer when we wallow in our relationship shortcomings. It makes us want to run and hide from God as they did in the Garden of Eden. Instead, run to God for His comfort, deliverance and healing. Focusing too much on what is wrong also causes us to question God's perfect wisdom.

If our relationship with Jesus is not working well, neither will our relationships with others work well.

We question Him in this manner: "Lord, you haven't given me 'this' and I really believe you wanted me to have 'it.'" Or, "I am so unhappy you are doing things 'this way.' Why won't things happen the way I think they should?" There are also questions like this: "Why do You allow the death of a relative, a child or valued member of the church, due to illness or worse yet, by a sudden accident?" All of these question God's perfect Love, Goodness, Wisdom and Authority.

"And we know that in all things God works for the good of those who love Him, who have been called according to His purpose" (Romans 8:28, NIV).

It does not say all things are good, but they do help develop us in our growth process. By the way, I believe all grumbling and complaining is against God. It basically questions God, "Are You sure You know what You are doing?" Our grumbling and complaining diminishes the quality of our relationship with God because we are focused on what He is doing (performance-based) rather than Who He is (relationship-based). We should seek His face (who He is) more than His hand (what He can do for us).

*"Glory in His holy name; let the heart of those who seek the Lord be glad. Seek the Lord and His strength; **seek His face continually**. Remember His wonderful deeds which He has done, His marvels and the judgments from His mouth"*
(1 Chronicles 16:10-12, emphasis by the author).

Reflections

1. What influences in this world push you toward perfectionism?

   _____

   _____

   _____

2. How would your life be different if you sought to be excellent or even satisfactory, instead of perfect?

   _____

   _____

   _____

3. Compare and contrast what causes you to run from God and what causes you to run toward God.

   _____

   _____

   _____

CHAPTER 29

QUIET OR NOISY?

None of the men who came up from Egypt,
from twenty years old and upward,
shall see the land which I swore to
Abraham, to Isaac and to Jacob;
For they did not follow Me fully.
(Numbers 32:11)

Why is God so quiet and the enemy so noisy? God is waiting for our voluntary submission to Him so that life may be lived the way He designed it to be. God has already said all He needs to say in His Word. However, He will say more by His Spirit if we listen and apply the truth He has already spoken to us. The world's way is, "show me and I will believe." God's way is, "believe Me and I will show you." To help us listen, in His mercy and lovingkindness, He has provided the Holy Spirit.

"But the Helper, the Holy Spirit, whom the Father will send in My name, He will teach you all things, and bring to your remembrance all that I said to you" (John 14:26).

There is an underlying, consistent current that runs through the Bible concerning God's provision, expectations and character. If we are intimately familiar with the Bible, we are equipped to hear the Holy Spirit remind us of God's tailor-made will and way for us. God wants us to choose to follow His ways instead of this broken world's "self" ways. This decision to follow His way is evidenced by our words, actions and attitudes. They indicate our true belief that He is Lord, God and King—worthy to be followed and obeyed. The benefits are out of this world! Read the Book and you will get to know the Author better.

The enemy (satan, our adversary), on the other hand, uses loud-mouthed bullying. The enemy tries to oppress us into submission through our well-trained, worldly side and our worldly, self-centered decision making. The enemy plants "lie-deas" into our mind, which are designed to move us toward fear, worry and hopelessness. This natural side is trained by a deteriorating world. We must be informed by the Living Word.

"And you will know the truth, and the truth will make you free" (John 8:32).

Provision has been made for us to live an abundant life in the fruit of the Spirit.

"But the fruit of the Spirit is love, joy, peace, patience, kindness, goodness, faithfulness, gentleness, self-control; against such things there is no law" (Galatians 5:22-23).

Exhibiting the fruit of the Spirit is not a rule to be followed; it is the supernatural overflow of His Spirit within you.

Exhibiting the fruit of the Spirit is not a rule to be followed; it is the supernatural overflow of His Spirit within you. Who in their right mind would not want these fruits of the Spirit? So, what is the "right" mind?

It is a mind set on the Spirit.

"The mind governed by the flesh is death, but the mind governed by the Spirit is life and peace. The mind governed by the flesh is hostile to God; it does not submit to God's law, nor can it do so. Those who are in the realm of the flesh cannot please God" (Romans 8:6-8, NIV).

It pleases God when we abide with Him through a real relationship with Christ Jesus. We may then make use of the gift of the Holy Spirit of Truth. God will bless us more than we can ask or imagine as we are taught and led by Him, instead of being jerked around by the world. The abundant life is a truth-centered life, not an opinion and feeling-centered life. Again, the benefits are out of the grasp of this world system and in the grasp of a loving and life giving Savior.

So, why is God so quiet? Because, "It is finished!" The work has been done at the cross of Christ. The world has been overcome and the enemy defeated. We can rest in God and His provision as we diligently seek Him.

"Seeing that His divine power has granted to us everything pertaining to life and godliness, through the true knowledge of Him who called us by His own glory and excellence" (2 Peter 1:3).

In other words, let's follow Him fully.

Reflections

1. Record some examples of what God may have already said to you which you may not have yet applied.

   _____

   _____

   _____

2. If possible, list and identify examples of how this world has pulled you down.

   _____

   _____

   _____

3. What prevents you from embracing God's way of living your life?

   _____

   _____

   _____

CHAPTER 30

SELF-MONSTER

*"Woe to you, scribes and Pharisees,
hypocrites! For you clean the outside
of the cup and of the dish, but inside they
are full of robbery and self-indulgence."*
(Matthew 23:25)

How big is your "self-monster?" Is it big enough to foolishly try to push God out of the command position He requests and deserves? He is in the command position whether we cooperate with Him or not. It goes all the way back to the book of Deuteronomy.

"Now it shall be, if you diligently obey the Lord your God, being careful to do all His commandments which I command you today, the Lord your God will set you high above all the nations of the earth" (Deuteronomy 28:1).

Then there is the other side of the coin—

"But it shall come about, if you do not obey the Lord your God, to observe to do all His commandments and His statutes with which I charge you today, that all these curses will come upon you and overtake you" (Deuteronomy 28:15).

Biblical history proved this standard of obe-dience to be impossible to uphold by human effort. The great events of the Old Testament were done by God manifesting His Presence through His people. In the New Testament, God sent us a Savior and gave us His Holy Spirit to be in us, not just with us.

> *"When the Helper comes, whom I will send to you from the Father, that is the Spirit of truth who proceeds from the Father, He will testify about Me"* (John 15:26).

The Holy Spirit, birthed in us by our soul-felt confession of Jesus Christ as the Son of God, will never lead us into the curses of disobedience.

It is the "self-monster" who leads us away from God's best for us. If your "me" has a capital "M," then your Lord has a lower case "L." Being self-led causes crushing calamity, disastrous disappointments and worrisome whining.

Self leads you away from God's guiding Spirit. Being self-led with our own understanding of the Bible (the logos or the written word) also fails miserably to demonstrate Christ's abundant life-giving love and power. It is very frustrating because

> *Being self-led causes crushing calamity, disastrous disappointments and worrisome whining.*

we expect being led by our own natural understanding to work well, but it just doesn't. The far superior option is a saved soul being led by the

Spirit of God (the rhema or God's spoken and living word). The written word never fails when interpreted by the Holy Spirit.

> *"Your ears will hear a word behind you, 'This is the way, walk in it,' whenever you turn to the right or to the left"*
> (Isaiah 30:21).

This rhema Word utilizes the logos Word applied to our always present need of guidance from the "Great I AM." The Spirit-led life creates opportunities for real fruit—fruit that remains and which bears more fruit. The self-led life creates plastic fruit—fruit with no seed and no nutrition. It is created by self-righteous "fruit inspectors."

> *"As it is written: 'God's name is blasphemed among the Gentiles because of you'"*
> (Romans 2:24, NIV).

May it be our heart's cry to be more like Him through following His Spirit. Then we can represent Him in an acceptable manner to those around us.

Reflections

1. Examine your life and consider some examples and results of the presence of the "self-monster" in your own life.

   _____

   _____

   _____

2. Explain why it is or isn't fair for God to set up this life with blessings for obedience and curses for disobedience.

   _____

   _____

   _____

3. List examples of the joy you have experienced through fruit-producing service to God. (Note: Do not let the "self-monster" try to condemn you if you have not yet experienced the joy of serving others.)

   _____

   _____

   _____

CHAPTER 31

SELF OR GOD?

*You will keep him in perfect peace,
whose mind is stayed on You:
because he trusts in You.*
(Isaiah 26:3, NKJV)

What are the "gods" in our minds we trade for the fellowship, peace and leadership which Jesus offers? What does your mind stay on most of the time? Is it situations, people you have to deal with, bills that need paying, broken things or broken people which need fixing? Is your mind stayed on your worries and cares of this world or on God and His leadership? Do not be deceived, what your mind dwells on is your true god. Is it going to be self or the one and only true and living God? Far too often my mind is stayed on me instead of "Thee"—my preferences, my opinions and my wants. Can you relate to this? There is no lasting peace there. God asks to be our one, true priority.

"You shall have no other gods before Me" (Exodus 20:3).

Make Him God, Lord and King of your mind.

"Humble yourselves before the Lord, and he will lift you up" (James 4:10, NIV).

Humble prayer lifts us up; anxious thoughts and worries in our prayer time diminish its quality. If not restrained, they turn our prayers into a "to do list" for God. But even so, God still definitely wants to hear our desires.

> *"Be anxious for nothing, but in everything by prayer and supplication with thanksgiving let your requests be made known to God. And the peace of God, which surpasses all comprehension, will guard your hearts and minds in Christ Jesus"* (Philippians 4:6-7).

Notice the conditions: be anxious for nothing, by prayer and supplication (an appeal, plea or petition). We must not forget "with thanksgiving!" With a vision of His greatness, mercy, compassion and all sufficiency, we will be thankfully confident, instead of the often-felt uneasiness that He may not be listening or answering our prayers. God always answers our prayers, but rarely in the way we think they should be answered. Where is the trust and confidence towards God in an impatient, my way, attitude?

God always answers our prayers, but rarely in the way we think they should be answered.

> *"But without faith it is impossible to please Him: for he that cometh to God must believe that He is, and that He is a rewarder of them that diligently seek Him"* (Hebrews 11:6, KJV).

Humbly seek Him in prayer and once you have found Him, lay down your burdens with confidence before a loving, caring, all powerful God. We can then have calm confidence in the middle of our storms—peace instead of worry. We will then overflow with thanksgiving as we see Him move on our behalf through His mysterious ways.

> *"Therefore humble yourselves under the mighty hand of God, that He may exalt you at the proper time, casting all your anxiety on Him, because He cares for you"*
> (1 Peter 5:6-7).

We have the privilege of casting or putting our cares on a God who is bigger than our issues, bigger than our perceived needs, bigger than circumstances, bigger than the reality we understand and observe around us. How "big" are your gods or how big is your God?

Reflections

1. Consider a few of the thoughts which repeatedly run through your mind.

   _____

   _____

   _____

2. If possible, analyze why it is easy or not easy to be thankful.

   _____

   _____

   _____

3. Evaluate what your life would be like if you cast all your anxiety on a God who loves you, created life and created the intended-to-be-perfect world around you.

   _____

   _____

   _____

CHAPTER 32

BREAKFAST OF CHAMPIONS

You prepare a table before me
in the presence of my enemies;
You have anointed my head with oil;
My cup overflows.
(Psalms 23:5)

Every day the Lord prepares a table before us. Our table is full of people, demands, choices, circumstances and time. There is a broad variety of "food" on this table. When Peter was on the roof and the two devout servants of Cornelius arrived at the gate, the Lord had given Peter a vision.

> *"And he saw the sky opened up, and an object like a great sheet coming down, lowered by four corners to the ground, and there were in it all kinds of four-footed animals and crawling creatures of the earth and birds of the air. A voice came to him, 'Get up, Peter, kill and eat!'"* (Acts 10:11-13)

The table of ministry to the Gentiles was set before Peter and he went to the home of Cornelius. Peter chose to eat the meat of obedience.

It is so easy when we wake up and look at the table of our day to grumble and complain as we eat the food of responsibilities and anxiety peppered with frustration and bitterness. Those are the foods of our negative, ungodly attitudes about the coming day. They will not lead us to a pleasant day. Why not look at the table set before us and start our day with a generous serving of sincere prayer and the fruit of the Spirit!

It is so easy when we wake up and look at the table of our day to grumble and complain.

"But the fruit of the Spirit is love, joy, peace, patience, kindness, goodness, faithfulness, gentleness, self-control; against such things there is no law" (Galatians 5:22-23).

A serving of this fruit seasoned with the sweetness of prayer is the true "breakfast of champions!" It will nourish your day with a positive, God-directed attitude. You will represent Christ well as your head is 'anointed with oil and your cup overflows.'

"O taste and see that the Lord is good; how blessed is the man who takes refuge in Him!" (Psalms 34:8)

If we have "tasted and seen that the Lord is good," He will, by His leadership, carry us away from the sickening table of our carnal, flesh nature. This table has deceivingly disguised maggoty, bitter, moldy and spoiled food. This food when eaten will make us sick to our stomach or even kill us. Remember, the Lord's table is prepared in the presence of our enemies. The food of a victorious and eternally significant day is offered to us by God, as He did through Peter's vision. We may eat as much of the eternally substantial food as the Lord offers from this day's table. Yet we will simultaneously loose the weight of the worries, cares and concerns of this world. We may then have the greatest joy in serving the food of the "Lord's table," thus enabling others to "taste and see that the Lord is good."

> *"But the worries of the world, and the deceitfulness of riches, and the desires for other things enter in and choke the word, and it becomes unfruitful"* (Mark 4:19).

Jesus is the Living Word and the Bread of Life. May the anointing oil of the Lord pour out on our heads and cause a flood of Living Water to flow out from us to others.

Reflections

1. Using the analogy of the "table" of your day, what do you normally eat from that table as you start your day?

   _____

   _____

   _____

2. At the end of the day, reflect on how your day began and the relationship between the beginning and the end of your day or days.

   _____

   _____

   _____

3. Explain and explore why it is or is not possible for you to live above the worries and cares of this world.

   _____

   _____

   _____

CHAPTER 33

WHO SAID?

*Take care, brethren, that there not be
in any one of you an evil, unbelieving
heart that falls away from the living God.
But encourage one another day after
day, as long as it is still called 'Today',
so that none of you will be hardened
by the deceitfulness of sin. For we have
become partakers of Christ, if we hold
fast the beginning of our assurance firm
until the end, while it is said: "Today if
you hear His voice, Do not harden your
hearts, as when they provoked Me. For
who provoked Him when they had heard?
Indeed, did not all those who came out of
Egypt led by Moses? And with whom was
He angry for forty years? Was it not with
those who sinned, whose bodies fell in the
wilderness? And to whom did He swear
that they **would not enter His rest**,
but to those who were disobedient?
So we see that they were **not able
to enter because of unbelief**.*
(Hebrews 3:12-19, emphasis by the author)

- **Who tells us abiding in the Lord is a complicated struggle?**

And WHO tells us:

"Grace and peace be yours in abundance through the knowledge of God and of Jesus our Lord. His divine power has given us everything we need for a godly life through our knowledge of Him who called us by His own glory and goodness. Through these, He has given us His very great and precious promises, so that through them you may participate in the divine nature, having escaped the corruption in the world caused by evil desires" (2 Peter 1:2-4, NIV).

- **Who tells us overcoming is an impossible battle of hopeless discouragement?**

And WHO tells us:

"I can do all things through Him who strengthens me" (Philippians 4:13).

This same One also tells us:

"Who is the one who overcomes the world, but he who believes that Jesus is the Son of God?" (1 John 5:5)

- **Who told us agreement with the validity of a truth is the same as a believing faith?**

And WHO tells us:

"Therefore, let us fear if, while a promise remains of entering His rest, any one of you may seem to have come short of it. For indeed we have had good news preached to

us, just as they also; but the word they heard did not profit them, because it was not united by faith in those who heard" (Hebrews 4:1-2).

We should not be so heavenly focused that we forget these now time-transforming truths. These truths lead us into an eternally significant life.

"But the word they heard did not profit them, because it was not united by faith in those who heard." (Hebrews 4:2b)

Reflection

1. Write a strategy to help you grasp, hold on to and live the life that is promised and available from these principles.

_____

_____

_____

_____

_____

_____

_____

_____

CHAPTER 34

FELLOWSHIP OR A SINKING SHIP?

*Therefore humble yourselves under
the mighty hand of God, that He may
exalt you at the proper time,
casting all your anxiety on Him,
because He cares about you ...
After you have suffered for a little while,
the God of all grace, who called you to His
eternal glory in Christ, will Himself perfect,
confirm, strengthen and establish you.*
(1 Peter 5:6-7, 10)

God asks us to cast all our cares on Him. Of course, He wants to hear our cares and concerns, but does He want us to dwell on them to the point that they are dominating our life throughout the day? Maybe these struggles, rooted mostly in the world, drown out His voice and His presence if we focus on the cares of this world instead of Him.

> *"For all that is in the world, the lust of the flesh and the lust of the eyes and the boastful pride of life, is not from the Father, but is from the world"* (1 John 2:16).

If the cares and concerns of this world consume us throughout the day, aren't we being led by the things of this world instead of by Him?

"For all who are being led by the Spirit of God, these are sons of God" (Romans 8:14).

If the cares and concerns of this world consume us throughout the day, aren't we being led by the things of this world instead of by Him?

This usually takes some painfully honest molding and making, similar to what a potter does to make or remake a beautiful vessel. Do we spend our time talking about what is wrong in our world or do we dwell on what is right with our God? Is God in control or are the worries of this world in control?

Let us be concerned with the things that concern God and then rest in Him. Let the Spirit take the lead so we may fellowship with Him bearing the fruit of eternal significance in our day. This also has the extra benefit of being accompanied by His joy and peace. The world is passing away, but the table is set before us.

"Rejoice in the Lord always; again I will say, rejoice! Let your gentle spirit be known to all men. The Lord is near. Be anxious for nothing, but in everything by prayer and supplication with thanksgiving let your requests be made known to God. And the peace of God, which surpasses all comprehension, will guard your hearts and your minds in Christ Jesus" (Philippians 4:4-7).

Jesus walked this earth in fellowship with the

Father. We are offered the same privilege—to walk with the same God who created the universe by His mighty power and holds the earth in its orbit. That same God holds us.

Jesus suffered greatly for a little while as He sacrificed His flesh on the cross. This fulfilled the Old Testament Law. His sacrifice provided the privilege for us to use our free will to choose the well-defended pathway of abiding with God.

Could it be that much of our own anxiety and "suffering" comes because our sinful nature is wiggling and squirming on our "cross," refusing to die?

> "Whoever does not carry his own cross and come after Me cannot be My disciple"
> (Luke 14:27).

Maybe we have not yet given up on the self-led, sin-based flesh nature and instead proclaiming as Jesus did "it is finished!"

> "After you have suffered for a little while, the God of all grace, who called you to His eternal glory in Christ, will Himself perfect, confirm, strengthen and establish you"
> (1 Peter 5:10).

Therefore, we desire to have no more self-confidence. Instead, we can have full confidence in Christ's care and control—internally, externally and eternally.

Reflections

1. Compare and contrast why it is or isn't possible for you to cast all your cares upon God?

_____

_____

_____

2. Read Philippians 4:4-7. Analyze your thoughts on what changes would occur in your life if these concepts truly played a greater part in your life.

_____

_____

_____

3. Evaluate yourself as to how much peace and contentment currently exists in your life.

_____

_____

_____

CHAPTER 35

COOPERATE

> *"We then, as workers together with Him also plead with you not to receive the grace of God in vain. For He says: 'In an acceptable time I have heard you, and in the day of salvation I have helped you.' Behold, now is the accepted time; behold, now is the day of salvation"*
> (2 Corinthians 6:1-2, NKJV)

How often are we cooperating with God according to His designs? Cooperation: "co" meaning together, "operation" meaning to function or work. Have we glossed over and denied His spoken truth which says:

> *"Do not be stiff-necked, as your ancestors were; submit to the Lord. Come to His sanctuary, which He has consecrated forever. Serve the Lord your God, so that His fierce anger will turn away from you"*
> (2 Chronicles 30:8, NIV).

By the way, coming to "His Sanctuary" is an everlasting, personal, spiritual place, not necessarily a physical place.

• **Is there steadfast peace?**

If not, there may be a lack of cooperation with God:

"Peace I leave with you; My peace I give to you; not as the world gives do I give to you. Do not let your heart be troubled, nor let it be fearful" (John 14:27).

- **Is there victory?**

If not, maybe there is a lack of cooperation:

"For everyone born of God overcomes the world. This is the victory that has overcome the world, even our faith" (1 John 5:4, NIV).

"But in all these things we overwhelmingly conquer through Him who loved us" (Romans 8:37).

- **Do we have the Fruit of the Spirit?**

Are these being practiced more and more: love, joy, peace, patience, kindness, goodness, faithfulness, gentleness, self-control? If not, there may be a lack of cooperation with God:

"I am the vine, you are the branches; he who abides in Me and I in him, he bears much fruit, for apart from Me you can do nothing" (John 15:5).

"Behold, I stand at the door and knock; if anyone hears My voice and opens the door, I will come in to him and will dine with him, and he with Me" (Revelation 3:20).

He seeks our voluntary cooperation. He desires our love. He will not force cooperation on us because He is not a God of bondage but a God of freedom. He gives us freedom to choose and receive peace, freedom from stress, freedom from worry, freedom to enjoy life and freedom to enjoy fellowship with others.

> "It was for freedom that Christ set us free; therefore keep standing firm and do not be subject again to a yoke of slavery" (Galatians 5:1).

He will not force cooperation on us because He is not a God of bondage but a God of freedom.

Living for the world is forced labor. Living for God is an adventurous journey.

Reflections

1. Describe a few positive examples where you voluntarily cooperated in an event or task.

   _____

   _____

   _____

2. Evaluate how your life might be different if you had more peace and more victory.

   _____

   _____

   _____

3. Formulate your own opinions on whether living for God is like an adventurous journey or living for the world is like forced labor.

   _____

   _____

   _____

CHAPTER 36

If

"If I shut up heaven that there be no rain, or if I command the locusts to devour the land, or if I send pestilence among My people; If My people, which are called by My Name, shall humble themselves, and pray, and seek My face, and turn from their wicked ways; then will I hear from heaven, and will forgive their sin, and will heal their land."
(2 Chronicles 7:13-14, KJV)

Notice the phrase "If I send pestilence among My people ..." Would a loving God send a pandemic or a plague? Yes, as an act of discipline and warning for those who have walked away from the Creator's standards of right and wrong.

"However, if you do not obey the Lord your God and do not carefully follow all His commands and decrees I am giving you today, all these curses will come on you and overtake you" (Deuteronomy 28:15, NIV).

- **"If my people who are called by My name ..."**

Today, that would be people who call themselves "Christians." Remember, Jesus said,

"Not everyone who says to Me, 'Lord, Lord,' will enter the kingdom of heaven, but only

the one who does the will of My Father who is in heaven" (Matthew 7:21, NIV).

- **"Shall humble themselves ..."**

If we do not humble ourselves to be led by Him, we will be humiliated by the world.

"The Lord will make you the head and not the tail, and you only will be above, and you will not be underneath, if you listen to the commandments of the Lord your God, which I charge you today, to observe them carefully" (Deuteronomy 28:13).

- **"And pray ..."**

We pray, but sometimes it is a repeated list of how we think God should do things or even prayers according to our will instead of His will. Or even worse, prayers where the heart is left out.

"Do not be quick with your mouth or im-pulsive in thought to bring up a matter in the presence of God. For God is in heaven and you are on the earth; therefore let your words be few" (Ecclesiastes 5:2).

- **"And seek my face ..."**

Only when we seek His face (to know who He is) more than we seek His hand (to see what He can do), will we have the hope of praying accord-ing to His will.

"Seek the Lord and His strength; seek His face continually" (1 Chronicles 16:11).

John also gave us this promise:

"This is the confidence which we have before Him, that, if we ask anything according to His Will, He hears us" (1 John 5:14).

Our spirit longs for this type of relationship and fellowship with God. It does not come naturally; it comes supernaturally.

- **"And turn from their wicked ways …"**

We don't have much chance of turning from our wicked ways which grieve him, unless we truly seek His face. We are quickly proud and this blinds us to our own wickedness.

We are quickly proud and this blinds us to our own wickedness.

"Because you say, 'I am rich, and have become wealthy, and have need of nothing,' and you do not know that you are wretched and miserable and poor and blind and naked" (Revelation 3:17).

- **"Then will I hear from heaven, and will forgive their sin, and will heal their land."**

We have much we need to respond to before He will heal our land. The proof of this need is the lack of healing in the land. This includes not only healing in the land surrounding me, but also healing of the "land" inside of me.

Reflections

1. Re-read Mathew 7:21 in the second paragraph above. Honestly and fearlessly meditate on what this verse says in relation to you and your life.

_____

_____

_____

2. What are your thoughts and feelings about humbling yourself under the guidance of an almighty, living and loving God?

_____

_____

_____

3. Honestly and fearlessly list some wicked ways you should turn from. If you are unable to list any, then maybe you should consider putting pride or denial on your list.

_____

_____

_____

CHAPTER 37

HEART TROUBLE

*Blessed are they which do hunger
and thirst after righteousness:
for they shall be filled.*
(Matthew 5:6, KJV)

Somehow, we have been fooled—fooled into thinking that we are "good" Christians because we have studied good Christian concepts and principles. We have even found some success at applying these principles to our lives and our thinking. Compared to many, our quality of life is good, our morality is good and our deeds are good. The Pharisees did all of these things as well. However, all of these do not automatically indicate a heart after God. Are you weary in your inner person from the chaotic, tiring life many call "Christianity?" Do we honestly hunger and thirst for His righteousness? Or, are we satisfied with our own performance-based and pride-based righteousness?

A heart after God realizes its own corruption. A heart after God realizes its own inability. A heart after God deeply depends on God and has given up on the detrimental distractions

A heart after God deeply depends on God and has given up on the detrimental distractions of the self-nature.

of the self-nature. Additionally, a heart after God is tired of the deep, inner discontent of a life lived according to its current level of understanding.

> *"Trust in the Lord with all your heart and do not lean on your own understanding. In all your ways acknowledge Him, and He will make your paths straight. Do not be wise in your own eyes; fear the Lord and turn away from evil"* (Proverbs 3:5-7).

How do we hunger and thirst after God and how do we win God's heart of blessing? The answer is true repentance or turning away from evil. We come to realize we are fruitless for the cause of Christ without His unshakable presence in our heart and mind, which compels us to turn from sin.

> *"I am the vine, you are the branches; he who abides in Me and I in him, he bears much fruit, for apart from Me you can do nothing"* (John 15:5).

The beginning of John 15 says:

> *"I am the true vine, and My Father is the vinedresser. Every branch in Me that does not bear fruit, He takes away; and every branch that bears fruit, He prunes it so that it may bear more fruit"* (John 15:1-2).

We cannot obtain His full righteousness; we can only put on His imparted righteousness by faith.

> *"And that you put on the new man which was created according to God, in true*

righteousness and holiness"
(Ephesians 4:24, NKJV).

I put on the "new man," which is Christ in me, by putting my own understandings, judgments and plans under His authority. What does this look like? It looks like peace. It looks like the end of worry and striving. It looks like contentment.

"Cease striving and know that I am God; I will be exalted among the nations, I will be exalted on the earth" (Psalms 46:10).

When people see us at peace, without striving and struggling, it exalts God. Getting our actions and attitudes right with God is not a comfortable process but life is infinitely and eternally better afterwards. A person with a heart after God, experiences the great I Am, in a moment-by-moment, ever-present fellowship. It is the absence of our own carnal opinions, judgments and never-ending string of the empty imaginations concerning the people and situations in our internal world and the external world around us. A heart after God totally trusts God. He becomes greater and more "real" to us than the natural world we see. A heart after God is characterized by much fruit—fruit that remains.

"Truly, truly I say to you, unless a grain of wheat falls into the earth and dies, it remains alone; but if it dies, it bears much fruit" (John 12:24).

Let us live to agree with God and die to our desire for people to agree with us.

Reflections

1. What would a stronger desire to live according to God's ways and His standards do for you?

    _____

    _____

    _____

2. List at least three ways you could find help in living for God.

    _____

    _____

    _____

3. Analyze your thoughts and feelings about the last sentence above concerning agreeing with God versus having people agree with you.

    _____

    _____

    _____

CHAPTER 38

PERFORMANCE

"Open confession is good for the soul."
Scottish proverb

In this perfectionist society we have set an unrealistic standard of being perfectly happy, having the perfect job, perfect spouse, perfect house, etc. This almost always leaves contentment as an unreachable future. If we just try harder, do better and become more perfect, we will then reach what we are seeking and find relief for the uneasiness of our soul. This perfectionism overlaid on Christianity may develop into what can be an unhealthy, obsessive desire for being aware of as many Biblical principles, truths and Scriptures as possible. It is masked in self-based performance and is a reflection of the common, modern-day error of the Pharisees.

The problem is, we see these truths and principles, but our hearts realize how far we fall short of living them. Then performance-based thinking screams at us: "You don't measure up! You're not good enough!" My first response is to forcibly apply these truths to myself because I need to do better ... maybe to prevent rejection. This is condemnation and it is the language of the enemy working through our flesh. Actually, a better choice is to throw ourselves into the mercy, love and grace of Jesus so we may utilize His power for the deliverance from striving in our own strength. This will change what we can never change using our own understanding and strength.

> *"Behold, God is mighty but does not despise any; He is mighty in strength of understanding. He does not keep the wicked alive, but gives justice to the afflicted"* (Job 36:5-6).

Additionally, Paul the Apostle wrote:

> *"And he said unto me, My grace is sufficient for thee: for My strength is made perfect in weakness"* (2 Corinthians 12:9a, KJV).

If our performance-based, "I-need-to-do-better" mentality persists without God's power to recreate us into "becoming better," then we will suppose all those around us need to also be doing better. If we're not careful, it will become a perceived mission from Christ to apply our own judgment and understanding of Biblical principles to the correction of others. This is most fiercely tested in our families. This performance-based "ministry" is called hypocrisy. It is defined in the Oxford Dictionary as "the practice of claiming to have moral standards or beliefs to which one's own behavior does not conform; pretense." It leads to a rejection of others for not holding up to the standards we perceive. God has set His standard before us. The growth of His standards in us is tailor-made by Him for each one of us personally.

The growth of His standards in us is tailor-made by Him for each one of us personally.

> *"How can you say to your brother, 'Brother, let me take out the speck [splinter] that is in your eye,' when you yourself do not see the log that is in your own eye? You hypocrite, first take the log out of your own eye, and then you will see clearly to take out the speck that is in your brother's eye"* (Luke 6:42).

The speck represents the sin of my brother. The log speaks of sitting in the seat of judgment. God has not qualified us to sit there and has never invited us to sit there. Judgment belongs to the Lord. It becomes very easy for us to judge but judging takes away our ability to love others as God loves them.

> *"By this all will know that you are My disciples, if you have love for one another"* (John 13:35, NKJV).

God has a more excellent way. God reminds me I am not a human doing, but a human being. He wants us to be more like Him and thus reveal His love and goodness to those around us. Let God put the puzzle pieces of our lives together as He uses His truth and His Spirit to fit them in their correct places, in the proper order and at the appropriate time. Confess your need for God.

Reflections

1. Give at least one example of when trying harder worked well in your life and when it didn't work well in your life.

   _____

   _____

   _____

2. Judge for yourself how a performance-based mindset possibly hinders showing grace and mercy toward others in your life.

   _____

   _____

   _____

3. Explain how letting God help you to become better would increase the quality of life for those you care about.

   _____

   _____

   _____

CHAPTER 39

GO AND LEAVE

"Jesus straightened up and asked her,
'Woman, where are they?
Has no one condemned you?'
'No one, sir,' she said. 'Then neither
do I condemn you,' Jesus declared.
'Go now and leave your life of sin.'"
(John 8:10-11, NIV)

When the woman caught in the act of adultery was told "go now and leave your life of sin," it was an empowered invitation to a mended life. Jeremiah the prophet said:

"Obey My voice, and I will be your God, and
ye shall be My people: and walk ye in all the
ways that I have commanded you, that it
may be well with you" (Jeremiah 7:23b, KJV).

Jesus intended it to be well with her but, for that to happen, she had to live out the command to "leave your life of sin." So it is with us. We must leave our habits of sin. One definition of sin means "missing the mark or the bullseye in archery." Only Christ's empowerment can enable us to turn and reach the abundant righteous life—not a self-righteous life, but a life of peace and calm in the midst of the storms. It is a life which goes well for us. This is a life which very few people achieve because they struggle to believe this is

God's desire and provision for them. It takes faith (complete trust and confidence in God) to receive this life which Christ empowers us to live.

The evidence this broken world gives us does not show God's true heart's desire for us. We have been trained by a broken world to live broken lives. The woman was not condemned by Jesus; neither did He disregard her sin. By His command she was empowered to leave her broken life which was not going well. Hopefully, she chose to accept the Lord's invitation and by faith to ignore the evidence of the world and the accusation of satan which said "there is no way, it is hopeless for you." Hopefully, you have accepted Christ's invitation.

The invitation was and is to turn to Christ and leave this world of condemnation: "Go now and leave your life of sin." How was this done for the woman and how is this done for us? Paul wrote to the Romans:

> *"There is therefore **now no condemnation** for those who are in Christ Jesus. For the law of the Spirit of life in Christ Jesus has set you free from the law of sin and of death"* (Romans 8:1-2, emphasis by the author).

Christ chose grace and mercy even though she was guilty and surely was feeling condemnation.

> *"Who shall bring a charge against God's elect? It is God who justifies. Who is he who condemns?"* (Romans 8:33-34a, NKJV)

He is still electing people today to remove condemnation from all who receive His offer of a mended life. Everyone is nominated and, when anyone chooses to run for "office," God elects them and invites them to become His child. The Old Testament law of sin, resulting in death, has been replaced with the New Testament Spirit of life offered to us by Jesus Christ—the Son of God who has given believers His Holy Spirit of Truth. There is no other advocate with such power and authority to grow us into the truth of a mended life where the puzzle pieces fit together well and the picture begins to make sense."

> *Everyone is nominated and, when anyone chooses to run for "office," God elects them and invites them to become His child.*

> *"Only acknowledge your iniquity, that you have transgressed against the Lord your God, and have scattered your favors to the strangers under every green tree, and you have not obeyed My voice, declares the Lord"* (Jeremiah 3:13).

The Holy Spirit has a voice to follow. It is the voice of conscience that will be heard and enabled when the voice of condemnation is removed.

> *"Those who live according to the flesh have their minds set on what the flesh desires; but those who live in accordance with the Spirit, have their minds set on what the Spirit desires"* (Romans 8:5, NIV).

Reflections

1. What in your life would you "go now and leave" if you were empowered to do so?

   _____

   _____

   _____

2. What would it require for you to have a life of calm in the midst of the storm?

   _____

   _____

   _____

3. How do you feel and what would you think about God having a "voice?" If you already agree that He has a voice, consider the ways you hear Him.

   _____

   _____

   _____

CHAPTER 40

I AM

"God said to Moses, 'I AM WHO I AM';
and He said, "Thus you shall say to the
sons of Israel, 'I AM has sent me to you ... '
'This is My name forever, and this is
My memorial-name to all generations.'"
(Exodus 3:14, 15b)

God is not constrained or limited by time. In Exodus, when He revealed Himself to Moses at the burning bush, He called Himself the Great "I AM." In the Bible, He declares what He has done and declares His promises of what He will do. This helps us in our time-confined life to trust and understand His story. If we believe in the Lord Jesus Christ, we personally know Him from the great things He has done in our past. And surely as believers, we should know Him with great expectation, through faith and hope, for the great things He will do in our future. When we reflect on His Lordship, we are considering Him in the present moment. He truly has been Lord of my past and He truly will be Lord over my future. But is He my Lord moment-by-moment as the great, ever-present "I AM"?

Jesus said:

*"**I am** the vine, you are the branches; he*

*who abides in Me and I in him, he bears
much fruit, for apart from Me, you can do
nothing"*
(John 15:5, emphasis by the author).

In addition to this verse, Jesus made several "I
AM" statements in the Books of John and Revelation. Abiding is a consistent, present moment-by-moment fellowship and awareness of the presence of the great "I AM." This is how Jesus walked.

*"But whoever keeps His word, in him the
love of God has truly been perfected. By
this we know that we are in Him: the one
who says he abides in Him ought himself to
walk in the same manner as He walked"*
(1 John 2:5-6).

We cannot change the past we have seen and cannot predict the future we have not seen. Other than the promises of God, all such prediction of the future is worrisome speculation and guesswork. However, we can trust and rest in the Great "I AM."

> *We cannot change the past we have seen and cannot predict the future we have not seen.*

As we drift into the past, He is not abiding there. He was there. But what I find in my own past, if I am not careful, is the condemning memory of poor choices, cruel words and hurts. We cannot abide in Him when we dwell morbidly in a "done" past. What about the future?

Paul said:

"Brethren, I do not regard myself as having laid hold of it yet; but one thing I do: forgetting what lies behind and reaching forward to what lies ahead, I press on toward the goal for the prize of the upward call of God in Christ Jesus" (Philippians 3:13-14).

Again, surely, He gives us a calling, goal, vision or dream of our future. But when I imagine myself in the future, I am not there yet. If I am not careful, many of the imaginations of the future are exaggerated, unproductive, empty and vain. His Lordship is a moment-by-moment, present-tense abiding as we live out His promises and His Word. This is how He builds our best future—by His power to deliver us and to produce growth, strength and victory in our present circumstances.

"Whom shall he teach knowledge? and whom shall he make to understand doctrine? them that are weaned from the milk, and drawn from the breasts. For precept must be upon precept, precept upon precept; line upon line, line upon line; here a little, and there a little" (Isaiah 28:9-10, KJV).

Wouldn't it be better to let Him carry and lead our moments so they are tied together into a future built by Him and not by ourselves? His guidance in moments of prayer without the invasion of the past or the worry of the future is the abiding place where we find the still waters, rest for our soul, guidance and the revelation of truth. Oh, how He wants us to go in prayer, always experiencing the abundant life He desires for us.

Reflections

1. Do an internet search using "Bible instances where Jesus said 'I AM the ... '" Specifically look in the Books of John and Revelation for insights and understanding.

   _____

   _____

   _____

2. What is your current strategy for abiding with the Lord and how could you improve or alter that strategy?

   _____

   _____

   _____

3. Think about why you are feeling encouraged (or discouraged) by the answers to the previous question.

   _____

   _____

   _____

CHAPTER 41

THE PROMISE KEPT

*And He Himself brought our sins in
His body on the cross, so that we might die
to sin and live to righteousness;
for by His wounds you were healed.
For you were continually straying like
sheep, but now you have returned to the
Shepherd and Guardian of your souls.*
(1 Peter 2:24-25)

The cross is where Jesus bore our sins and not His own, for He had none. When this sinless God/man died, the battle between good and evil, righteousness and sin was given a new dimension. His natural body died unfairly, slain by this world, contrary to God's law. In Genesis, the first and foundational book of the Bible, we find this decree:

> "The Lord God commanded the man, saying, 'From any tree of the garden you may eat freely; but from the tree of the knowledge of good and evil you shall not eat, for in the day that you eat from it you will certainly die'" (Genesis 2:16-17).

The knowledge of good and evil, combined with Adam and Eve's free will, led to rebellion and sin, which brought death. Jesus, on the other hand, having the perfect knowledge of good and evil, used His free will to choose only the good.

So, because God keeps every promise and is a God of truth, for Jesus to die would break God's promise of sin being the cause of death. It is not possible for the God of truth who created everything to lie, break a promise or to alter the truth. Sinful men in a sinful world killed the body of sinless Jesus. God thus fulfilled the law concerning the Old Testament sacrificial system. This opened the door for a new and better way.

> *Sinful men in a sinful world killed the body of sinless Jesus.*

Paul said in the book of Romans:

"For the wages of sin is death, but the free gift of God is eternal life in Christ Jesus our Lord" (Romans 6:23).

Though He was tempted, Jesus committed no sin (Hebrews 4:15; 7:26). Jesus had earned no wages for death. So, the God of heaven was obliged by His own law to bring Jesus back to life after He was unjustly put to death by the world. Jesus descended into an undeserved hell and took away the authority of death.

"He who descended is Himself also He who ascended far above all the heavens, so that He might fill all things" (Ephesians 4:10).

The resurrection that followed this act of injustice brought us the New Covenant of forgiveness and peace with God. The requirement in the law of the Old Testament sacrifice of animals was forever satisfied by the shed blood and sacrifice of Jesus on the cross.

> *"For the preaching of the cross is to them that perish foolishness; but unto us which are saved it is the power of God"* (1 Corinthians 1:18, KJV).

Genesis also speaks of the days of Noah:

> *"Then the Lord saw that the wickedness of man was great on the earth, and that every intent of the thoughts of his heart was only evil continually"* (Genesis 6:5).

It is so easy for us to choose wickedness. We are trained by the world and drawn toward evil by our broken nature. God knew we lacked the power to lead a righteous life. We need the cross. Jesus did not stay on the cross; sin stayed on the cross. Our sins belong on the cross.

> *"And He was saying to them all, 'If anyone wishes to come after Me, he must deny himself, and take up his cross daily and follow Me'"* (Luke 9:23).

Put the sins of your weak, selfish flesh on the cross. If you keep them, they will lead you to death. Carry the cross of your own sins as a reminder of what you have left behind on the cross of Christ. Choose Jesus who overcame sin and death for you.

Our lives as adults are primarily defined by

the results of what we choose. Choose the resurrection of Christ, which gives us the power and desire to turn from our own evil and move toward His righteousness.

"He who is steadfast in righteousness will attain to life, and he who pursues evil will bring about his own death"
(Proverbs 11:19).

The life promised when we diligently strive for righteousness will lead us away from evil and toward eternal life. This pursuit of righteousness produces the fruit of the Spirit.

"But the fruit of the Spirit is love, joy, peace, patience, kindness, goodness, faithfulness, gentleness, self-control; against such things there is no law" (Galatians 5:22-23).

Death is promised to those who pursue evil. The habit or practice of evil also leads to the death of God's promised blessings on your life. It also leads to eternal death.

"Now the deeds of the flesh are evident, which are: sexual immorality, impurity, sensuality, idolatry, sorcery, enmities, strife, jealousy, outbursts of anger, disputes, dissensions, factions, envying, drunkenness, carousing, and things like these, of which I forewarn you, just as I have forewarned you, that those who practice such things will not inherit the kingdom of God"
(Galatians 5:19-21).

Reflections

1. Some of Jesus' last words from the cross were "It is finished." Considering what we are to do with our sins, explain how our sins could be brought back off the cross and into our lives again.

   _____

   _____

   _____

2. Compare and contrast a righteous versus an evil life and describe the power which leads toward one or the other.

   _____

   _____

   _____

3. In view of the above, what better choices could you make and what better results might you expect?

   _____

   _____

   _____

CHAPTER 42

MISTAKEN MINDSETS

*"And he came into all the district around
the Jordan, preaching a baptism of
repentance for the forgiveness of sins;
as it is written in the book of the words of
Isaiah the prophet, 'The voice of one crying
in the wilderness, 'Make ready the way
of the Lord, make His paths straight.'"*
(Luke 3:3-4)

God is crying out in the wilderness of this world for us to "make ready the way of the Lord." We make ourselves ready when we realize the need to do things differently. This is repentance. Once we accept Christ for who He is, we will walk on fewer and fewer crooked paths. John the Baptist said: "Make His paths straight!" Let His resurrection power and sacrifice for you empower you to exchange your previous, flesh-driven life for a better and more abundant life. This repentance opens the door of God's blessings. Without agreeing with Him about our poorly functioning life, we will not be able to follow Him. If we follow Him, our life will function better, become straighter and more focused on His purposes. It is an intricate, *It is an intricate, individualized, adventurous and sometimes difficult path.*

185

individualized, adventurous and sometimes difficult path. I was not stronger than satan, who was
destroying me, but Jesus in me is stronger.

*"Greater is He who is in you than he who is
in the world"* (1 John 4:4b).

He will lead us to victory if we accept His better way.

There are two common mindsets which can
hinder God's loving provision of "abundant life"
being poured out on us:

One—if we allow our conscience to keep rat-
tling the bones of the past. This will cause our
walk with the Lord to be impaired by guilt and
shame. With guilt and shame, we are basically saying: "Surely Lord, You are still angry with
me about my sin." This contradicts God's amazing love and grace for us and is a sure recipe for a
sense of worthlessness. It is written:

*"Therefore, there is now no condemnation
for those who are in Christ Jesus ... in order that the righteous requirement of the
law might be fully met in us, who do not
live according to the flesh but according to
the Spirit"* (Romans 8:1,4, NIV).

A loving God, as a loving parent, is not angry at
our unrighteousness. He is brokenhearted when
we choose sin because of the disabling results we
will receive. Ask yourself: What more does God
need to do for you to be able to accept His forgiveness and receive the freedom from sin, guilt
and shame? He loves us, but hates evil. He has

made provision by His strength and power to turn us away from the practice of evil!

Two—the crippling attitude of being bound by multiple sins and thinking we are "OK" because He is a God of love and forgiveness. This also is not the righteous, abundant life which Jesus died for us to enjoy.

"Act as free men, and do not use your freedom as a covering for evil, but use it as bondslaves of God" (1 Peter 2:16).

By His power and our cooperation, we are free from self-destructive behaviors.

The Apostle John wrote:

"If we confess our sins, He is faithful and righteous to forgive us our sins, and to cleanse us from all unrighteousness"
(1 John 1:9).

We are not forgiven and cleansed from the sins which we continue to commit or practice while asking for forgiveness over and over. He empowers us to break the cycle of those sins so He may erase them—forever. God loves us too much to leave us just as we are. Suffering the consequences of choosing evil and seeking the results of choosing God's better way both produce a type of "godly sorrow in us." Paul explained how godly sorrow convicts us and leads us to true repentance but the sorrow of the world leaves us feeling hopeless, helpless and condemned.

"For the sorrow that is according to the will of God produces a repentance without regret, leading to salvation, but the sorrow of the world produces death"
(2 Corinthians 7:10).

Reflections

1. What does it mean to "make your path straight?"

_____

_____

_____

2. Describe the discouragement or reasoning concerning the difficulty of making your path straight.

_____

_____

_____

3. Analyze whether or not God's forgiveness erases and or softens the consequences of your poor choices.

_____

_____

_____

CHAPTER 43

DESOLATE OR FORTIFIED?

*"So they will say, 'This land that was
desolate has become like the garden of
Eden; and the wasted, desolate, and ruined
cities are now fortified and inhabited.'"*
(Ezekiel 36:35, NKJV)

As we come to more fully know Christ and the manner of life He desires for us, "the ruined cities" of our broken past become "fortified and inhabited." The landscape of our lives has become more like Eden, because we can "walk with God in the cool of the day" (Genesis 3:8). This happens as the Holy Spirit of Christ rules and reigns in our lives. He moves us toward the knowledge of the truth and away from the "knowledge of good and evil." He provides the plan and the power to turn away from rebellion against God, which leads to death.

> *"So also it is written, 'The first man, Adam, became a living soul.' The last Adam became a life-giving spirit"*
> (1 Corinthians 15:45).

In Eden, there was no question about God's rightful place of authority and no question of His love ... but it didn't stay that way.

God asked the first Adam, "Who told you that you were naked?" Jesus, the last Adam, asks us the same thing in the present tense as we strive to walk victoriously.

"For all of you who were baptized into Christ have clothed yourselves with Christ" (Galatians 3:27).

Notice we have been clothed with Christ. So, we are no longer spiritually "naked." Jesus has clothed us in Himself with His righteousness.

"It is because of Him that you are in Christ Jesus, who has become for us wisdom from God—that is, our righteousness, holiness and redemption" (1 Corinthians 1:30, NIV).

He has grafted us into Himself. We are invited to share His characteristics and follow His empowered plan of turning away from our fleshly, sin-filled, self-trained life. Now, we can walk with Him in a new way of walking. In this process, we learn to abide in Him. When we make Him more important than our issues, struggles, and self-agenda, we can then cross back into another privilege of Eden—we find God meeting our every need as we walk with Him. Quality prayer time and Bible study lead us away from a broken world and toward a mended life.

Quality prayer time and Bible study lead us away from a broken world and toward a mended life.

As we apply these principles, God will not need to ask as He

asked Adam, "Where are you?" (Genesis 3:9). Today, He might ask His children with head tilted and
mild curiosity, "Where are you ... and why in the
world are you way over there?" Through Christ,
we have regained the privilege of unbroken fellowship with the Lord—the great I Am! Our reality is altered with more of Eden in our hearts. The
wasted, desolate, and ruined "cities" of our life
are now fortified and healthily inhabited. Circumstances, life, and even people, are much more
bearable as He leads us with our eyes focused on
God.

I picture Eden as heaven on earth. That is
until Adam and Eve's eyes were opened to the
knowledge of good and evil. Ever since, mankind
has been confused by our free will choices.
We see more of heaven when the lures of this
world become less appealing. They are replaced
by the joy and deliverance found in a guiltless
relationship of obedience with our LORD, Savior,
God and King. It is a relationship which provides
cleansing and healing.

Reflections

1. Re-read our key verse. What in your life feels desolate and uninhabited?

   _____

   _____

   _____

2. Evaluate what the term "clothed in Christ" could mean for your life.

   _____

   _____

   _____

3. Imagine and record parts of "Eden" you would enjoy visiting with your life.

   _____

   _____

   _____

CHAPTER 44

QUEST-BASED LIVING

My children, with whom I am again
in labor until Christ is formed in you—
but I could wish to be present with you now
and to change my tone of voice,
for I am perplexed about you!
(Galatians 4:19-20)

The object of Christianity is to become more like Christ. The world needs more people who represent Him well. People should see something in us which will make them desire Christ as their Lord and Savior. How much of us looks, acts and thinks like Him? If you don't recognize Him in yourself, He may not recognize Himself in you.

> *"Not everyone who says to Me, 'Lord, Lord,' will enter the kingdom of heaven, but he who does the will of My Father who is in heaven will enter. Many will say to Me on that day, 'Lord, Lord, did we not prophesy in Your name, and in Your name cast out demons, and in Your name perform many miracles?' And then I will declare to them, 'I never knew you; depart from Me, you who practice lawlessness'"* (Matthew 7:21-23).

If we are in the habit of practicing "lawlessness," He doesn't know us and we don't really know Him. There are many works we may do in our own strength, but the only way we can avoid lawlessness is to be led by the truth. The Holy Spirit reminds us of the truth and will never lead us to lawlessness. Ask yourself, "How much happens, or has happened in my life, which can only be explained by the power of God in my life?" The challenge of this question is multiplied in intensity by this verse:

> *"Truly, truly I say to you, the one who believes in Me, the works that I do, he will do also; and greater works than these he will do; because I go to the Father"*
> (John 14:12).

Is this true? Do we believe this? How does this play out in your life? How far is God willing to take us in this quest for Christ? The better question is: "How willing are we to go?"

> *"Then I heard the voice of the Lord, saying, 'Whom shall I send, and who will go for Us?' Then I said, 'Here am I. Send me!'"*
> (Isaiah 6:8)

Being led by God richly speaks to our heart. It is a relationship which fully answers all the deep questions of our hearts in this life journey. There is, however, a depth of living which you cannot reach without a personal relationship with the Living

> *Being led by God richly speaks to our heart. It is a relationship which fully answers all the deep questions of our hearts in this life journey.*

God. It is a relationship which daily, moment-by-moment, gives you wisdom for living. When Jesus truly comes into your life and you hunger and thirst for more of Him, it is an adventurous, quest-based life. You will know God, and He will know you! This is because you will be working together with Him in full cooperation.

> *"Blessed are they which do hunger and thirst after righteousness: for they shall be filled"* (Matthew 5:6, KJV).

> *"Therefore, brethren, be all the more diligent to make certain about His calling and choosing you; for as long as you practice these things, you will never stumble; for in this way the entrance into the eternal kingdom of our Lord and Savior Jesus Christ will be abundantly supplied to you"* (2 Peter 1:10-11).

If we don't truly know Him and His Spirit, our life will not have the power it takes to be more like Him. He wants us to be real, not an imitation.

Reflections

1. What are a few of the most un-Christlike characteristics you think people may see in you or that you may see in yourself? (Guilt and shame are not to color this list but, rather, the promise of deliverance as you agree with God that you want to see these changed. He offers the power which we lack for these changes.)

_____

_____

_____

2. Compare, for yourself, the difficulty or simplicity of needing God's power to change your life for the best.

_____

_____

_____

3. Evaluate the effect of pride in your life when considering the above principles.

_____

_____

_____

CHAPTER 45

CHOICES AND RESULTS

*"Jesus said to him, 'You shall love the Lord
your God with all your heart, with all
your soul, and with all your mind.'
This is the first and great commandment.
And the second is like it: 'You shall
love your neighbor as yourself.'
On these two commandments hang
all the Law and the Prophets.'"*
(Matthew 22:37-40, NKJV)

When will we begin to love the Lord our God with all our heart, soul and mind? When will we desire Him, obey Him, seek Him and submit to Him? As we do these, we are inviting Him to mend any and all aspects of our lives which have been broken by this world. A whole new perspective opens up to us.

"Therefore if any man be in Christ, he is a new creature: old things are passed away; behold, all things are become new" (2 Corinthians 5:17, KJV).

God is a restoring and restructuring builder driven by love and a desire to bless us. He is grieved when our free-will choices take us away from His provision for us to have a better life. Many go so far as to make their lives a living hell by their own choices. We may even choose to hate God because of the results of our own poor choices or the poor choices of others around us. All choices have consequences. If you are not getting good results, you can either play the blame game or take responsibility and make better choices.

The verse above says, "all things become new." This is not an easy process. However, it is well worth doing. It takes moving toward a healthy valuing of ourselves and moving away from an enemy-inspired, condemning opinion of ourselves. It also requires a healthy and respectful love toward God who wants so much for you to receive His love and blessings.

Why not choose to love the Maker and Creator of everything and enjoy His re-creation? Jesus called loving God the first and greatest commandment because it results in a great life! Surely you will still have struggles, trials and tribulation in this broken world; but you will also have peace and calm in the midst of the storms of life. Jesus said:

> *"But the Helper, the Holy Spirit whom the Father will send in My name, He will teach you all things, and bring to your remembrance all that I said to you. Peace I leave you; My peace I give to you; not as the world gives do I give to you. Do not let your heart be troubled, nor let it be fearful"*
> (John 14:26-27).

Why not just do what He says? There is a good reason the Holy Bible significantly outnumbers any other book ever distributed. Ask the Spirit of God to help you interpret correctly the Word of God. God's Word interpreted by our own understanding can and has produced many catastrophes individually, corporately and historically.

Notice, the key verse above also says, "And the second is like it: 'You shall love your neighbor as yourself.'" Be willing, courageous and honest enough to stop doing what hurts you and start doing what helps you. You will not learn this from the world. You will not learn this from religion. Many have religion-based head knowledge about "God," but many do not truly "know" the living God as a heart reality. They just know about a god. Love and respect yourself enough to let the God who created you show you how to truly love and be loved.

Be willing, courageous and honest enough to stop doing what hurts you and start doing what helps you.

Loving your neighbor is the overflow of accepting and experiencing God's love for you. Receive the new life God offers. Become built up by God instead of torn down by the world. Then find the joy of helping others who will also become mended in this broken world.

Conclusion

Both categories of God's promises are true: the promises for blessings and the promises for curses. God spoke through Moses to Israel saying:

> *"I call heaven and earth to witness against you today, that I have set before you life and death, **the blessing** and **the curse**. So choose life in order that you may live, you and your descendants, by loving the Lord your God, by obeying His voice, and by holding fast to Him; for this is your life and the length of your days, that you may live in the land which the Lord swore to your fathers, to Abraham, Isaac, and Jacob, to give them"* (Deuteronomy 30:19-20, emphasis by the author).

God the Creator, in His wisdom and authority, has established this world and how it functions. It is best if we learn from Him, cooperate with Him and live life under the protection of His truth. He wants to prosper us and give us hope. He wants to give us an abundant life. The other choice is co-operating with satan and getting the results of an angry, bitter enemy who wants to steal from us, kill us and destroy us.

Jesus declared:

> *"**I AM** the door; if anyone enters through Me, he will be saved, and will go in and out*

*and find pasture. The thief comes only to steal and kill and destroy; I came that they may have life, and have it abundantly. **I AM** the good shepherd; the good shepherd lays down His life for the sheep"* (John 10:9-11, emphasis by the author).

Everyone strives to grow in their understanding of life and the world around them. An important fact to understand is this: There is a God who is supreme and in charge of everything. The enemy is not even close to being in the same league as God Almighty. What this means is, if you want the enemy's destruction and devastation in your life, do things other than God's way. Do it your own way but you won't like the results. The enemy (satan) has been luring people into trying to be their own gods and doing things their own way since the beginning. In fact, the enemy got kicked out of heaven because he rebelled and wanted to be his own god. Isaiah recorded it like this:

> *"How you have fallen from heaven,*
> *O star of the morning, son of the dawn!*
> *You have been cut down to the earth,*
> *you who have weakened the nations!*
> *But you said in your heart,*
> *'I will ascend to heaven;*
> *I will raise my throne above the stars of God, and I will sit on the mount of assembly in the recesses of the north.*
> *I will ascend above the heights of the clouds;*
> *I will make myself like the Most High.'"*
> (Isaiah 14:12-14)

We (and the world) have gotten terrible results by living life according to our own inadequate understanding and ungodly standards. And this pretty much answers the questions: "Are God's ways best?" or "isn't it OK to be my own god and do what I want?" These eternal questions posed by satan have been answered but are still working themselves out individually, in our world and in time. The world's system has proven that when left to be our own "gods," the planet and mankind greatly suffer. God's ways and submission to His authority are the best choice. One way leads to life, the other way leads to death.

If you are getting unsatisfying results in your life, examine yourself to see where the problem lies. My greatest growth in the Lord has come from looking at all my circumstances as God's personalized instruction plan for me to grow in Him. The enemy does not have dominion over a Believer/Disciple. That would take away our free will. Therefore, the enemy can only get in where he finds a breach in the walls of Christ's righteousness around me—the walls which we build in cooperation with God's provision for us.

Because of this building process, enemy activity becomes a compass to point to where I need God's help and deliverance to build the wall stronger. We seek God and His Word to repair the breaches in the walls protecting us. A fortified city has strong walls. When the damage done by the enemy opens a pathway through the wall, there is a truth of God to be believed, to repair and to bring us back into fellowship with God. But there also is a lie the enemy wants us to believe, a lie to make us doubt God. If we do so, we end up giving in to satan's attack and his desire to steal from us, kill us and destroy us.

Examine yourself: what truth do you not believe? What wrong action, failure of character or ungodly attitude does God want to deliver you from? The Lord will close up the breaches in the wall as you believe and trust Him more. Closing the breaches in the wall will usually require a change in us before a change in the circumstance happens. Invite and cooperate with God to win the battle inside and then He will fight and win the battles on the outside for us.

"Take care, brethren, that there not be in any one of you an evil, unbelieving heart that falls away from the living God. But encourage one another day after day, as long as it is still called 'Today,' so that none of you will be hardened by the deceitfulness of sin. For we have become partakers of Christ, if we hold fast the beginning of our assurance firm until the end, while it is said, 'Today if you hear His voice, do not harden your hearts, as when they provoked Me.' For who provoked Him when they had heard? Indeed, did not all those who came out of Egypt led by Moses? And with whom was He angry for forty years? Was it not with those who sinned, whose bodies fell in the wilderness? And to whom did He swear that they

would not enter His rest, but to those who were disobedient? So we see that they were not able to enter because of unbelief" (Hebrews 3:12-19).

You see, we are able to enter into God's rest because our belief in God has pushed past the enemy-inspired lies and the human ways which we learned from the world. The god of this world (satan) is truly not our primary enemy; God has defeated him for us through Christ's perfect life.

Please hear me out. Our primary enemy (as believers) is what remains of our enemy-inspired, self-centered, unloving, wants-its-own-way, and craves-the-things-of-this-world self-nature. It is our broken, sinful nature that gives place to the enemy. We cannot win this battle with an "I hope so" or "I think so" faith. It grows to be an "I know so" faith as you move forward. The battle against the enemy is won by faith, trust and obedience to God and His Word. When we are born again, we are supposed to stand tall in God and be overcomers. We are to be wise to the enemy's schemes and we are supposed to be victorious.

Think about it. In the Old Testament, the Israelites always won great and miraculous victories when they were in good standing with God by trusting and believing Him. God winning victories is not any different for us in this present world. In fact, we have the advantage of a new and improved Covenant through the work of the cross. The enemy was defeated two thousand years ago. It is about time that we believed it and live in it!

In the Bible, I have never found where God's people were boasting about the enemy's dominion and power in their life, as if their faith was in what the enemy was able to do. Their hope and "boasting" was in the God of Abraham, Isaac and Jacob and what He did and is able to do.

> *"He again fixes a certain day, 'Today,' saying through David, after so long a time just as has been said before, 'Today if you hear His voice, do not harden your hearts.' For if Joshua had given them rest, he would not have spoken of another day after that. So there remains a Sabbath rest for the people of God"* (Hebrews 4:7-9).

Consider this: God's own "day of rest" (according to Genesis) came after the work of Creation. Our rest also comes after the work—after the work of the cross. The spiritual work of the cross in our life gives us the ability to have the Spirit of God actually living within us.

Oh, believer, do not quench the Spirit of God, but be filled with the Holy Spirit's Power and Love —the power and love which overcomes death, hell and the grave. Be confident in your growth as the enemy finds fewer and fewer ways to deceive you. Doing this will bring honor and glory to God. Be transformed by the renewing of your mind and the renewing of your faith.

"Cease striving and know that I AM God; I will be exalted among the nations, I will be exalted in the earth" (Psalms 46:10).

Trust God fully. It is the best choice you will ever make. It breaks the heavy yoke of bondage and replaces it with a yoke that is easy and light.

Jesus said:

"For My yoke is easy and My burden is light" (Matthew 11:30).

The primary burden of this new yoke is to abide in Him and walk with Him as He guides you in His ways. He provides the help and power for you to do this through your faith. You must not lean on a carnal, flesh-based understanding.

"Trust in the Lord with all your heart and do not lean on your own understanding. In all your ways acknowledge Him, and He will make your paths straight. Do not be wise in your own eyes; fear the Lord and turn away from evil" (Proverbs 3:5-7).

Do not be quick to make your own decisions and judgments. Wait on the Lord as He helps you think and respond to the people and events of your life. Walk in prayer. Strive to do and remember these things always and you will receive abundantly more from God than you could ever hope or imagine. In doing this you will have God's perfect peace that passes all understanding and the strength to weather any storm. The Master Builder will use you to be an agent of change to those around you and bring honor and glory to

His name. You will rejoice in the eternal harvest you will reap from a God-centered life.

Man at the Beach

My wife, April, my son, Jesse, and I were visiting a friend on the coast of North Carolina during my break from teaching school. It is my custom, while at the beach, to rise early and enjoy the magnificent demonstration of God's power, where ocean meets land. Gazing over the sea oats and across the sand to the sun peaking over the horizon, the shimmering waters and the prismatic colors of the sky are a soul-refreshing sight. It is, for me, the most unmistakably, awe-inspiring setting to spend time with God in prayer.

While earnestly praying, a man walking past on the lonely beach caught my attention. I sensed in my spirit the Lord saying, "Go, walk down to the beach and speak to that man." My assumption was to give him a word of encouragement. I immediately jumped up and briskly walked to the beach and came alongside him.

Well, actually, like most of us, when we feel like God may be speaking, it just seemed too weird. While continuing to pray, the unction kept returning and grew to the point of submission and obedience. By that time the man was hundreds of yards down the beach.

Walking to the beach, I was grieved about probably missing God's timing ... again. The man's tracks in the sand reminded me of the poem,

"Footprints." "Well God, if you want me to talk to him, You will have to let me catch up."

Immediately, the man bent down to pick up something, then he turned around and started walking toward me. It was a little unsettling. Walking toward him, my mind started racing, wondering what soul-probing question could be uttered to start this "God-ordained," encouraging conversation. As we met, I told him, "I was praying and felt compelled to come and encourage you." He endearingly said, "I'm good, how about you?" Somehow his simple question had the ability to pierce my own soul. It brought to my remembrance a core concern of what I sensed may be God's calling on my life, one of the very things I was praying about just a few minutes earlier. "I'm wrestling with a few things," was my response.

Then, my soul probing question came out, "What do you do for a living?" Wow! The man, whose name I never asked, replied, "I am a teacher." "Me too!" was my eager reply. "Are you a Christian?" The man calmly, yet firmly, said, "Yes, I am." The stranger then told me the story of a testimony he had heard.

It was about a young man in high school. Most people thought he would never amount to anything. The young man was disrespectful toward authority and the law. He was proudly self-centered and did pretty much whatever he wanted. The results later on were not as expected. As it turned out, the 25-year high school reunion found this man in a healthy relationship with the Lord and leading a successful ministry.

"I have a ministry disguised as a middle school teacher! What do you teach?" "Everything; I am a substitute," was his reply.

This plainly dressed, middle-aged man appeared to have such a caring and compassionate character. I was at ease to share my heart. "I have a burden for 'Christian' make-believers, believers and nonbelievers who fail to be led by the Spirit of God ... not that I have a great understanding of the Spirit-led life. I am ashamed to say after twenty years of salvation, I am still seeking more Spirit leadership." He replied, "Better now than never. Just do what the Lord says." Immediately, the dream, or maybe calling, to write a book on moving from carnal to Spiritual Christianity leapt inside of me.

"Well, I am going to go up here. I promised my children some seashells." The man left, and as I turn to walk away, a single shell, half buried in the surf, caught my attention. It was a medium-sized, curiously-colored conch shell.

To my utter amazement, as I pulled it out of the sand, it was actually a whole conch shell, not a bleached white partial shell. It was the first whole conch I had ever found on the beach! The words "I promised my children some shells" trumpeted inside me. When I turned to catch sight of the man, he was GONE!

Then I remembered:

"Do not neglect hospitality to strangers, for by this some have entertained angels without knowing it" (Hebrews 13:2).

There was no way, to my rational mind, that this man could have traveled the distance to any of the nearest beach houses in the time it took me to pick up that shell. With my heart pounding, I felt like the men who encountered Jesus on the road to Emmaus—

"They said to one another, 'Were not our hearts burning within us while He was speaking to us?'" (Luke 24:32a)

My heart was burning inside of me, so I journaled this experience.

To this day, that shell holds a special place at my writer's desk. As I return to the account of this experience from my journal, the nature of this encounter is made ever so clear. First, remember, I thought of the poem "Footprints" while I was looking at the man's singular set of footprints in the sand. There are many versions, but to paraphrase the closing stanza:

"He whispered:

My precious child, I love you and will never leave you. During your times of trials and testing, When you saw only one set of footprints, It was then that I carried you!"

Believe me, I needed some carrying at that time. Next, relaying my desire to encourage the man on the beach, his response was "I'm Good."

As I look back, Mark 10:18 comes to mind. "Why do you call Me good? No one is good except God alone." Then there was the question: "What do you do for a living? "I am a teacher," was the answer. Is not Jesus the definitive teacher? Next came, "Are you a Christian?" What was his response? "Yes, I am!"

The Scripture says:

"God said to Moses, 'I AM WHO I AM'; and He said, 'Thus you shall say to the sons of Israel, 'I AM has sent me to you.'"
(Exodus 3:14)

After this followed the testimony he shared. I now realize the testimony was a reflection of my own life! Then, when I asked, "What do you teach?" His reply was, "Everything, I am a substitute!" Won't Jesus teach us everything we need to know, if we accept His substitutionary death? Next came the statements, "Better now than never" and "Just do what the Lord says." This made me think of this Scripture verse:

"But I gave them this command: Obey me, and I will be your God and you will be my people. Walk in obedience to all I command you, that it may go well with you"
(Jeremiah 7:23, NIV).

What is God's call, except a call to obedience and action to His Holy Spirit's leadership? This obedience results in the many blessings God longs to give.

Most amazing to me was finding the conch

shell—"Well, I'm going up here. I promised my children some shells." What are the chances? Moments after his statement, the first ever whole conch shell, which I had hoped to find for all my life, was lying at my feet, half buried in the surf. Doesn't God give us these unexplainable "coincidences" which speak of His personal involvement in our lives?

Finally, there was the sudden disappearance. This sealed it for me. God had personally visited me through this stranger on the beach.

And nearly a decade later, I have retired from teaching and taken to writing. My first step in this book was to review and summarize the years of my journaled journey toward a better understanding of God. The amazing thing is this act of obedience has revived and ignited my faith. Maybe, that's the result of "just doing what the Lord says"—a reignited faith!